LIEUTENANT SCHWATKA SHOWING THE ESKIMOS THE
"ILLUSTRATED LONDON NEWS."
Page 23

THE SEARCH FOR FRANKLIN.

A NARRATIVE OF THE AMERICAN EXPEDITION
UNDER LIEUTENANT SCHWATKA,
1878 to 1880.

WITH ILLUSTRATIONS,
FROM ENGRAVINGS DESIGNED BY THE ARTIST OF THE EXPEDITION.

London:
T. NELSON AND SONS, PATERNOSTER ROW.
EDINBURGH; AND NEW YORK.

1899

Contents.

	INTRODUCTION,	9
I.	EARLY EXPERIENCES OF THE EXPLORING PARTY,	19
II.	THE STORIES OF THE NATIVES,	40
III.	RETRACING THEIR STEPS,	66
IV.	SEAL AND WALRUS HUNTING,	76
V.	SAFE HOME,	94
VI.	LIEUTENANT SCHWATKA'S PERSONAL NARRATIVE,	97
VII.	THE VOYAGE OF THE "JEANNETTE,"	113

List of Illustrations.

LIEUTENANT SCHWATKA SHOWING THE ESKIMOS THE "ILLUSTRATED LONDON NEWS,"	*Frontispiece*
MAP OF SLEDGE JOURNEYS AND SEARCHES,	8
DOWN HILL,	27
DISCOVERY OF LIEUTENANT IRVING'S GRAVE,	51
VIEW IN SUMMER, KING WILLIAM'S LAND,	63
ON THE SALMON CREEK,	77
REINDEER-HUNTING IN KAYAKS,	91
CROSSING SIMPSON STRAIT IN KAYAKS,	103
BREAKING UP OF THE ICE,	107

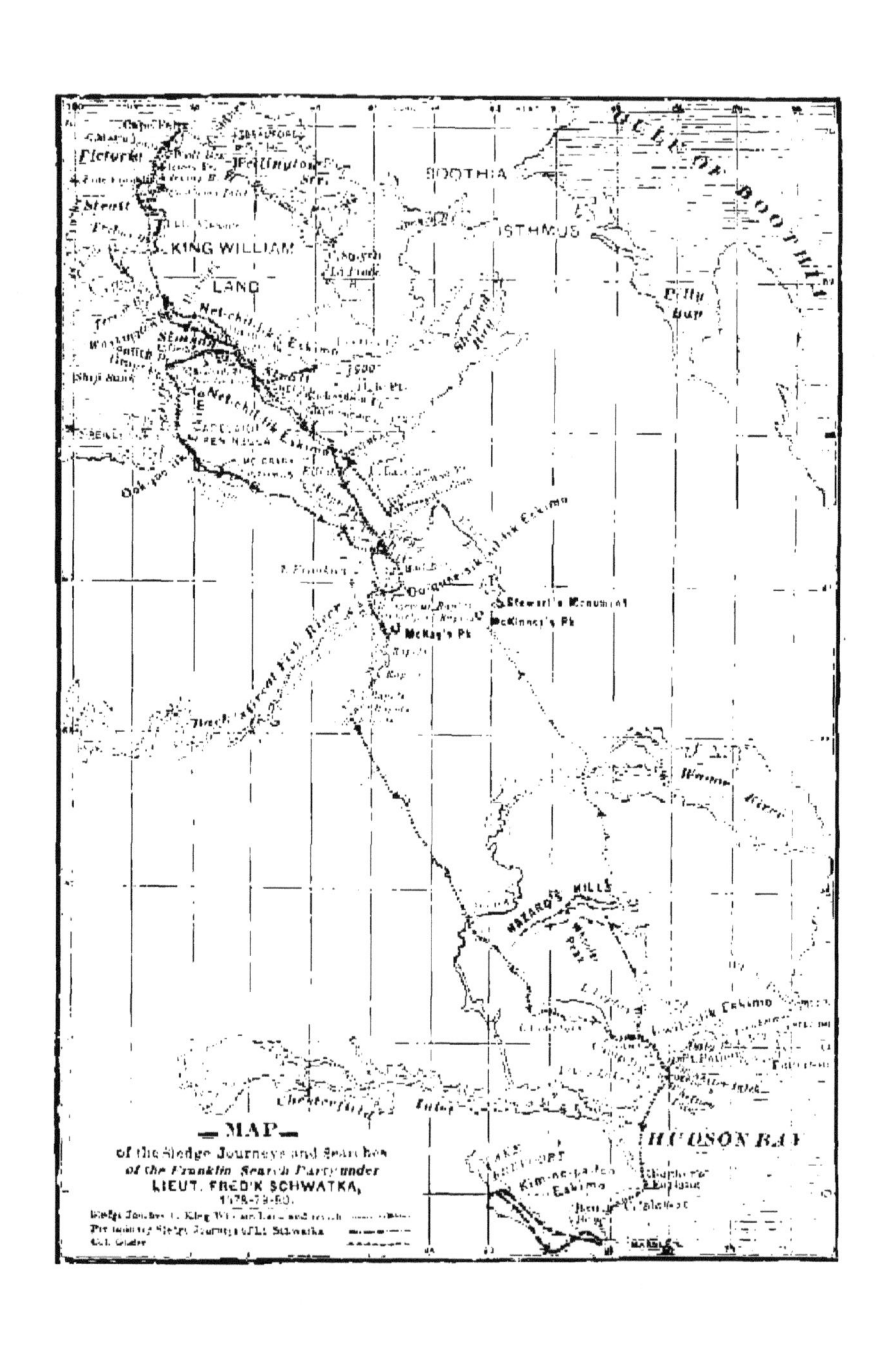

—MAP—
of the Sledge Journeys and Searches
of the Franklin Search Party under
LIEUT. FRED'K SCHWATKA,
1878-79-80.

THE SEARCH FOR FRANKLIN.

INTRODUCTION.

SIR JOHN FRANKLIN had already earned a high reputation as an Arctic explorer when, in the spring of 1845, he was placed by the British Admiralty at the head of an expedition designed to prosecute the search after a North-West Passage,—that is, a channel of communication between Baffin Bay on the west coast and Behring Strait on the east coast of North America. No better choice could have been made; for he was a man of high scientific acquirements, of large experience, of undaunted courage, and of blameless character. The two ships placed under his command were the *Erebus* and the *Terror*, both of which had already encountered the perils of the Arctic seas: in the former Franklin hoisted his own flag, the latter was in charge of Captain Crozier. Carefully equipped, provisioned for three years, and carrying one hundred and thirty-seven picked men as their crews, the two ships sailed from the Thames towards the end of May. On the 8th of June they left the Orkney Islands, and directed their course towards the extreme point of Greenland, known as Cape Farewell. A month later they dropped anchor for a while among an archipelago of rocky islets on the east side of Baffin Bay. After a brief rest, Franklin pushed forward across the bay to Lancaster Sound, his course being much impeded, however, by the pack-ice, which had not yet broken up. His ships were "spoken" about this time by a Hull whaler, the *Prince of Wales*, to whose master Franklin and Crozier reported that all were well, and all confident of successfully accomplishing their high enterprise. That same evening, the 26th of July, the ice gave way; and the *Erebus* and the *Terror*, steering to the north-west, plunged into Lancaster Sound. And then a cloud, as it were, descended upon them; a darkness and a mystery: they passed into the frozen wastes of the Arctic World, and disappeared as completely as if the sea had suddenly engulfed them. Of late years, some memorials of them, as we shall see, have been discovered; but even now the record is imperfect, and the whole story of the fate of Franklin's expedition will never be revealed to the curious gaze of mankind.

It was not expected that any news of the progress of the voyagers would reach England until the summer of 1846, or even the spring of 1847; and no apprehensions, therefore, arose as to their safety until the latter date had passed. When the summer of 1848 came, without intelligence, a natural anxiety seized upon the public mind; and when the winter went by, and still nothing was heard of Franklin and his men, the anxiety deepened into alarm. At length the Government resolved to send expeditions in search of the missing heroes. One was despatched under Sir James Ross, and another under Sir John Richardson; but both failed to discover the slightest traces of their course. A third expedition, under Captains Moore and Kellet, started from Behring Strait, and worked towards the east: in their boats they got as far as the mouth of Mackenzie River; but their endeavours were fruitless. Then, in the spring of 1849, the Government offered a reward of £20,000 to any private adventurers, of any nation, who should discover and relieve the wanderers; and Lady Franklin, a woman of noble devotedness and heroic patience, organized several relieving parties out of her own and her friends' resources. In 1850 no fewer than ten expeditions, under Sir James Ross, Rae, M'Clure, Osborn, Penny, Austin, Collinson, Forsyth, Ommaney, and De Haven, were searching amid the frozen wilds of the far North for Franklin and his companions.

The instructions given to Franklin by the Admiralty had directed him to pass through Lancaster Sound into Barrow Strait, thence to Cape Walker, and from Cape Walker to make his way into Behring Strait by any possible channel. The general opinion was that he had sailed to the west of Melville Island (or Peninsula), and then been caught in the ice among the islands which stud that portion of the Polar Sea. And it was assumed, but on very insufficient grounds, that he would be engaged in an effort to cross the ice and reach one of the Hudson Bay Company's settlements or some whaling-station.

Dr. Rae, therefore, started for Banks Island, whence he proposed to reach Cape Walker. Captains Collinson and M'Clure undertook the eastern route, by way of Behring Strait. Others sailed for Baffin Bay to follow up Franklin's supposed route; others steered for various points of Banks Land and Boothia—these last including an American expedition, fitted out by Mr. Henry Grinnell of New York, and consisting of the brigs *Advance* and *Rescue* (May 1850).

Two of these numerous searching-parties were to a certain limited extent successful. In August 1850 Captains Austin and Penny, who had gained the eastern entrance of Wellington Channel, were forced, by the accumulated ice, to take shelter in a great bay in the rear of Beechey Island. On the 23rd, a boat's crew from Captain Ommaney's ship, the *Assistance*, landing on one of the headlands of the bay, were surprised to meet with signs of a former visit of Europeans. Under the cliffs of Cape Riley they found the obvious ground-plan of a tent, scraps of rope and canvas, and a quantity of birds' bones and feathers; but nothing appeared to identify these memorials with the missing explorers. On hearing of their discovery, however, Captain Penny resolved, in conjunction with Lieutenant de Haven of the Grinnell Expedition, to undertake a careful search in the neighbourhood of Wellington Channel. While they were lying under the west point of Beechey Island, some of their men were allowed to go ashore. On landing, they strolled about until they reached a low projecting spur which stretches to the north. They ascended the acclivity, gained the summit, and were then seen from the ships to rush towards a dark object and gather round it in an excited assemblage. That another "find" had been made everybody at once recognized, and all hands made a simultaneous dash for Beechey Island. There, on the point, rose a pyramidal cairn, the base of which was formed by a series of preserved meat tins filled with gravel and sand, while another series was arranged so as to taper upwards to the summit, where was fixed the broken shaft of a boarding-pike. But no record seemed to connect it with Sir John Franklin. What now? What are those strange objects yonder, on the northern slope? They rush eagerly towards them, to stop—hushed, breathless, silent—before three graves, on the rude wooden tablets of which are roughly carved the significant words "*Erebus* and *Terror*."

During the winter several vessels lay at Beechey Island, and sent out sledge-parties in all directions. These added much to our knowledge of the configuration of the Arctic basin, but made no further discovery of Franklin relics; and it came to be accepted as a fact that, after leaving Wellington

Channel, Franklin must have taken a south-westerly course. Dr. Kane, the surgeon accompanying Lieutenant de Haven's expedition, came, however, to a different conclusion. Falling in with what he supposed to be traces of heavily laden sledges, he formed the opinion that, after the ice had broken up in 1846, Franklin had pushed to the north from Cape Riley, and from Wellington Channel steered into the Polar Sea. Accordingly, the *Advance* made her way as far as possible in this direction, conquering a thousand obstacles; but no more relics were then discovered. Afterwards, however, a record found at Point Victory vindicated the accuracy of Kane's conjecture, and showed that Franklin *had* attempted that course, but had been driven back by dangers and difficulties of an insuperable character.

So earnest was Dr. Kane's belief in his theory that he lost no opportunity of urging upon his countrymen the propriety of despatching another expedition. His exertions, in 1853, were crowned with success; and on the 30th of May he left New York, in Mr. Grinnell's brig the *Advance*, with a company of eighteen men and officers. His idea was that the Greenland peninsula extended far to the northward, and in all probability approached the Pole much nearer than any other land; that, therefore, it afforded an easier access either to the east or the west than Wellington Channel; and hence he resolved on an overland route in as direct a line north as the nature of the country permitted.

Dr. Kane reached Melville Bay on the 27th of July. On the 5th of August he passed the so-called Crimson Cliffs of Sir John Ross; and next day came in sight of the two great snow-capped headlands, Cape Alexander and Cape Isabella, which command the entrance to Smith Sound. On Littleton Island he established a depôt of stores for use on his return voyage. Thence he pushed forward beyond Cape Lifeboat Cove to a beautiful sheltered bay, which he appropriately named Refuge Harbour. Adopting this as his permanent station, he took with him seven of his men, and in his best and lightest whale-boat proceeded farther north to find some place where a winter encampment might be formed, with a view to the despatch of sledge-expeditions in the following spring. After a careful exploration of the coast, he considered it advisable to return to Refuge Harbour and winter there, as it offered greater advantages than any other spot. On Butler Island he erected a store-house, a dog-house, and an observatory; but he and his men lived and slept on board the ship. It is unnecessary for us to dwell on the harsh experiences of an Arctic winter; they have been so often described that every reader will be familiar with them. Kane and his companions were heartily glad when the long darkness was at an end, and the sun reappeared above the horizon on the 21st of February. The darkness is harder to bear than the cold; though what *this* is, when the thermometer sinks to 75° below freezing-point, the reader may imagine!

In the course of the summer of 1854 Dr. Kane discovered the Great Humboldt Glacier,—the huge frozen river which connects the American continent with Greenland. "Its curved face, from Cape Agassiz to Cape Forbes, measures fully sixty miles in length, and presents a grand wall or front of glistening ice, kindled here and there into dazzling glory by the sun. Its form is that of a wedge, the apex lying inland, at perhaps 'not more than a single day's railroad travel from the Pole.' Thus it passes away into the centre of the Greenland continent, which is occupied by one deep unbroken sea of ice, twelve hundred miles in length, that receives a perpetual increase from the water-shed of vast snow-mantled mountains. A frozen sea, yet a sea in constant motion, rolling onward slowly, laboriously, but surely, to find an outlet at each fiord or valley, and to load the waters of Greenland and the Atlantic with mighty icebergs, until, having attained the northern limit of the land it overwhelms, it pours out a mighty congealed torrent into the unknown Arctic space."

Dr. Kane, with a portion of his crew, remained a second winter in the ice, suffering terribly from scurvy and insufficiency of provisions; but manifesting through every trial a noble patience and indomitable energy. With the return of spring returned his desire to discover some traces of the Franklin expedition or of its survivors: but nearly all his dogs had perished; sledge-journeys were impossible; and there was nothing to be done but to attempt the homeward journey. Abandoning their brig, which was inextricably ice-bound, they set forth on their perilous way—thirteen hundred miles of ice and water lying between them and North Greenland. We wish we had room to trace the record of this remarkable enterprise; but it must suffice to say that it was successfully accomplished, and that on the 4th of August they arrived, half-starved, weary, wan, and enfeebled, at the settlement of Upernavik. They had failed to discover Sir John Franklin, but they had considerably enlarged our knowledge of the Polar World.

In 1857, another expedition* was fitted out by Lady Franklin, and placed under the command of Captain M'Clintock, who in a small screw-schooner, the *Fox*, wintered in Melville Bay, and in the following summer resuming his voyage, slowly felt his way into Bellot Channel,—the waterway which leads from Regent Inlet into the great Arctic Sea whose waters wash the American coast from Great Fish River to Behring Strait. Here he was caught in the ice, and compelled to winter. In February 1859 he set out on a sledge-expedition, and at Cape Victoria, on the west shore of Boothia (in lat. 69° 50' N. and long. 96° W.), had the happiness to come upon traces of the lost. There, from some Eskimos, he learned that, a few years before, a ship had been shattered

* This was the eighteenth British expedition despatched in search of Franklin.

by the ice-pack off the north coast of King William Land; that all her people, however, had safely reached the land, and travelled across to the Great Fish River; but that there they had died. Acting on the hint thus obtained, M'Clintock and one of his officers, Lieutenant Hobson, proceeded to explore King William Land, M'Clintock on the eastern and Hobson on the western side. The former, from King William Land, struck across to Montreal Island, and doubling the estuary of the Great Fish River, visited Point Ogle and Barrow Island. He found no fragments of wreck, no human skeletons; but from the natives he obtained, by barter, a number of relics of the ill-fated *Erebus* and *Terror*. To complete the circuit of King William Land he turned to the north-west, and landing on the north side of Simpson Strait, made for the cairn erected by Simpson in 1839 upon Point Herschel. When within ten miles of it, he came upon a bleached skeleton. It was probably that of one of the stewards of the expedition, who, having fallen behind his retreating companions, had perished of cold and famine in the solitude.

From Cape Herschel to the westernmost point of King William Land the traces of the Eskimos had effaced those of Franklin and his followers; but thenceforward to Cape Felix, M'Clintock met with painful evidence of their sufferings and of the calamities that had overtaken them. In conjunction with Lieutenant Hobson he effected an extensive survey of the whole territory, and arrived at the following results:—

The two exploring ships passed their first winter at Beechey Island, in the spot discovered by Captains Penny and Austin; but they had previously explored Wellington Channel as far as 73° N., and sailed down again into Barrow Strait, between Cornwallis and Bathurst Lands. In 1846 they appear to have steered through Peel Channel, until beset by the ice off King William Land, on the 12th of September. In May 1847 Lieutenant Graham Gore and Mr. des Vœux landed, and erected a cairn a few miles south of Point Victory, depositing in it a document which stated that on that day all were well, with Sir John Franklin in command. Within a month, however,—that is, on the 11th of June,—that great navigator died; happily for him, as he thus escaped the terrible trials which overtook his followers. The ice did not break up, and they were doomed to a third winter in the Polar wilderness. It proved fatal to nine officers and fifteen men. On April 22, 1848, the survivors, one hundred and five in number, under the command of Captains Crozier and Fitzjames, abandoned their ice-bound ships, and started for the Great Fish River.

At the cairn, and all around it, Hobson discovered a quantity of clothing and other articles, which, after a brief experience of only three days, the sufferers had evidently found a burden too great for their enfeebled energies.

From this point to a spot about midway between Point Victory and Point Herschel, Hobson found little of importance; and skeletons and relics all lay deeply embedded in the snow. At this midway station, however, the top of a piece of wood projecting from the snow was seen by Lieutenant Hobson; it proved to be a portion of one of the boats. This stood upon a heavy sledge, and contained a couple of skeletons. The one in the bottom of the stern-sheets was covered with a quantity of cast-off clothing; the other, in the bows, seemed to have been that of some unfortunate who had crept there to look out, and in that position had fallen into his last sleep. Close at hand stood a couple of guns, loaded and ready cocked, probably for use against wild animals. Around this boat lay another heap of cast-off articles; and it is assumed that the party in charge of her were returning to the ships, having found their strength unequal to the terrible journey before them. The stronger members of the crews, meanwhile, went on their dreary way.

"The point," says Sherard Osborn, "at which the fatal imprisonment of the *Erebus* and the *Terror* in 1846 took place was only ninety miles from the spot reached by Dease and Simpson in their boats in 1838-39, coming from the east. Ninety miles more of open water, and Franklin and his gallant crew would have not only won the prize they sought, but reached their homes to wear their well-earned honours. It was not to be so. Let us bow in humility and awe to the inscrutable decrees of that Providence who ruled it otherwise. They were to discover the great highway between the Pacific and the Atlantic. It was given them to win for their country a discovery for which she had risked her sons and lavishly spent her wealth through many centuries: but they were to die in accomplishing their last great earthly task; and, still more strange, but for the energy and devotion of the wife of their chief and leader, it would in all probability never have been known that they were indeed the first discoverers of the North-West Passage."

The expedition under M'Clintock which had obtained this information was the last sent out from England in search of Franklin and his followers.

CHAPTER I.

EARLY EXPERIENCES OF LIEUTENANT SCHWATKA'S EXPLORING PARTY.

SOME regret was expressed by enthusiasts in the matter of Arctic exploration that, on the return of the *Fox*, no steps were taken by the British Government to obtain fuller particulars of the fate of Sir John Franklin and his companions, and to pay the last marks of respect to the remains of so many gallant Englishmen. But at that time the Government seems to have grown weary of Polar adventure, and it discountenanced every fresh effort or proposal in that direction. In America, however, the subject was not allowed to be forgotten. The late Captain Hall, a veteran explorer, pursued a series of laborious investigations among the Eskimos, or Innuits, as they prefer to call themselves, and eventually ascertained, from the evidence they furnished, that one of Franklin's ships, with five of her crew still on board, had actually accomplished the North-West Passage, and that, after having been abandoned by her crew, she was found by the Innuits (in the spring of 1849) near O'Reilly Island, lat. 68° 30' N., and long. 99° 8' W., imprisoned in the ice.

During his long residence among the Innuits, Hall collected some hundred and fifty relics of the ill-fated expedition, in the shape of articles which had belonged either to the ships or their officers. It would seem that Captain Crozier and a companion were living as late as the autumn of 1864.

For several years reports were received through American whalers wintering at, or visiting, the northern part of Hudson Bay, that books and other memorials of Franklin were known to exist in certain districts, to which the Eskimos would be willing to conduct the white man; and in one instance, about three years ago, it was affirmed that some of Franklin's men had crossed the Boothia Isthmus, and reached a point on Melville Peninsula in the neighbourhood of Fury and Hecla Strait. Relics of the expedition, it is said, were there deposited in a cairn. These reports found little credence in England, but in the United States many persons were less incredulous, and among others a gallant officer, Lieutenant

Schwatka, was so influenced by them that he resolved on the difficult and even dangerous enterprise of testing, and, if possible, confirming their accuracy.

With three companions, he was landed by a whaler, in August 1878, near Chesterfield Inlet, which, as a glance at the map will show, lies at the northern end of Hudson Bay. The stores, provisions, and equipments which he had brought with him from the United States he disembarked at a point named Camp Daly (in lat. 63° 40′ N.), resolving to winter there among the natives, to adopt, as far as possible, their habits and mode of living, and to persuade them in the spring to accompany his party in whatever direction he should decide to travel.

Lieutenant Schwatka soon ascertained that there was no foundation for the story of Franklin records existing eastward of Boothia, and that in fact it unquestionably referred to King William Land. Thither, accordingly, he resolved to penetrate as soon as the winter had passed away—that is, he made up his mind to traverse a tract of wholly unknown country for a distance of about three hundred and fifty miles as the crow flies; and then, on reaching King William Land, to undertake an elaborate search of its coasts, which could not involve less than six hundred miles of travel; to remain until the winter set in, so that he might recross the frozen strait between the island and the mainland (as he was not provided with a boat); and finally, to retrace his steps to Hudson Bay during the depth of an Arctic winter. It is needless to dilate on the arduous and adventurous character of such an expedition. To conceive it was a bold thing, to execute it a bolder; for Schwatka and his companions had little to depend upon except the natural resources of a country of which they knew nothing, and were fully conscious that the realization of their scheme would occupy a twelvemonth. However, to use their own words, their "igloo life"* during the winter inured them to the climate, so that, though they often found the cold intensely disagreeable, they avoided the evil consequences which have assailed many expeditions and made Arctic travel so dangerous. Numerous sledge journeys taught them how to clothe and otherwise defend themselves against the extreme cold; and they also became acquainted with Innuit or Eskimo fare, so that when compelled to subsist entirely upon it they did not experience the distaste of those to whom it comes as a repulsive novelty. In other words, during their winter

* An "igloo," or Eskimo hut, is built of frozen snow.

residence at Camp Daly they became thoroughly acclimatized.

The Eskimos of this locality emigrated some eight years ago from the shores of Repulse Bay. They are a simple-minded people, and easily amused. On one occasion their wonder was excited by some conjuring tricks which Mr. Gilder performed, but they showed still greater astonishment when for the first time shown an illustrated newspaper, and the pictures fairly riveted their gaze.

At eleven o'clock on the morning of the 1st of April 1879, the adventurers began their journey, accompanied by thirteen Eskimos, including women and children, with several kayaks, or canoes, and three heavily-laden sledges drawn by forty-two native dogs. These sledges carried about a month's provisions for the whole party, consisting principally of bread and meat landed from the whaler, and their store of firearms. To these, which appear to have been of the best description, they probably owed their great success in procuring game, as well as their personal security from the native tribes with whom they came in contact.

At Winchester Inlet they struck to the north-west, and took up their line of march upon the frozen waters of Conery River. The sun was setting when they halted about ten miles from Camp Daly and built two igloos, or snow-huts, one of which was occupied by the family of an Eskimo named Toolooah, and the four white men; the other, by the remainder of the party. After the first night, however, three igloos were always erected, Joe and Ishnark, his father-in-law, building a separate one for themselves and their families. Here we may particularize the members of the expedition.

White men: — Lieutenant Frederick Schwatka, United States army, commander; W. H. Gilder, second in command; Henry W. Klutschak; and Frank Melms.

Eskimos:—" Eskimo Joe," interpreter; Nupshark, his wife; Toolooah, dog-driver and hunter; Toolooah-elek, his wife, and one child; Equeesik, dog-driver and hunter; Kutchunuark, his wife, and one child; Ishnark, Karleko, his wife, and Koomana, their son; Mit-cotelee and Owawork, Equeesik's brothers, aged respectively about twenty and thirteen.

The loads carried in the three sledges weighed about five thousand pounds on the day of starting; but as a large portion consisted of walrus meat both for dogs and for people, they were materially lightened from day to day. In addition to the walrus meat, the provisions included:—Hard bread, five hundred pounds; pork, two hundred pounds; compressed corned beef, two hundred pounds; corn starch, eighty pounds; oleomargarine, forty pounds; cheese, forty pounds; tea, five pounds; coffee, forty pounds; molasses, twenty pounds. This, it will be seen, was not more than one month's rations of "civilized food" for seventeen people, and the supply was nearly exhausted by the time our adventurers reached King William Land. Their main dependence, therefore, was on the game of the country they were about to explore; and the extent to which they availed themselves of this resource may be inferred from the fact that in the course of the expedition they killed five hundred and twenty-two reindeer, besides musk oxen, Polar bears, and seals.

On the 8th of April they came upon an interesting natural curiosity—a frozen waterfall, about twenty-five feet in height, glittering in the sunlight with ripples of crystal, and sparkling as if incrusted with myriads of flashing gems. From a distance it looked like a mountain torrent which had suddenly been arrested in its progress by some magic spell and hardened into stone. Tracing its course for a short distance from the shore, Lieutenant Schwatka found a shallow brook which had frozen in a level at the top of the hill, forcing the water to the right and left until it spread in a thin sheet over the face of the rock for a breadth of about fifty feet. Successive layers of ice were thus created, and, on the whole, a novel and beautiful effect was produced.

On the 14th, the thermometer, for the first time, rose above freezing-point at mid-day; and the white men remaining in camp while the hunters fared ahead to look for a better road, they profited by the brief interval of rest to dry their stockings. For be it known that one of the special discomforts of Arctic travel arises from the perspiration with which the exercise of walking covers the traveller's fur stockings. At night they freeze, and it is not a pleasant sensation to put bare feet into stockings filled with ice. But we suppose there never was an evil to which one could not get accustomed, and even to this uncomfortable experience the Arctic traveller is, after a while, resigned. The warmth of the feet soon thaws the ice, and then a wet stocking is nearly as warm as a dry one, except in the wind.

On the 15th, while descending a hilly range, they experienced a startling incident. The first sledge had got down safely, though not without difficulty; but when the second had reached half-way, the dogs, in a

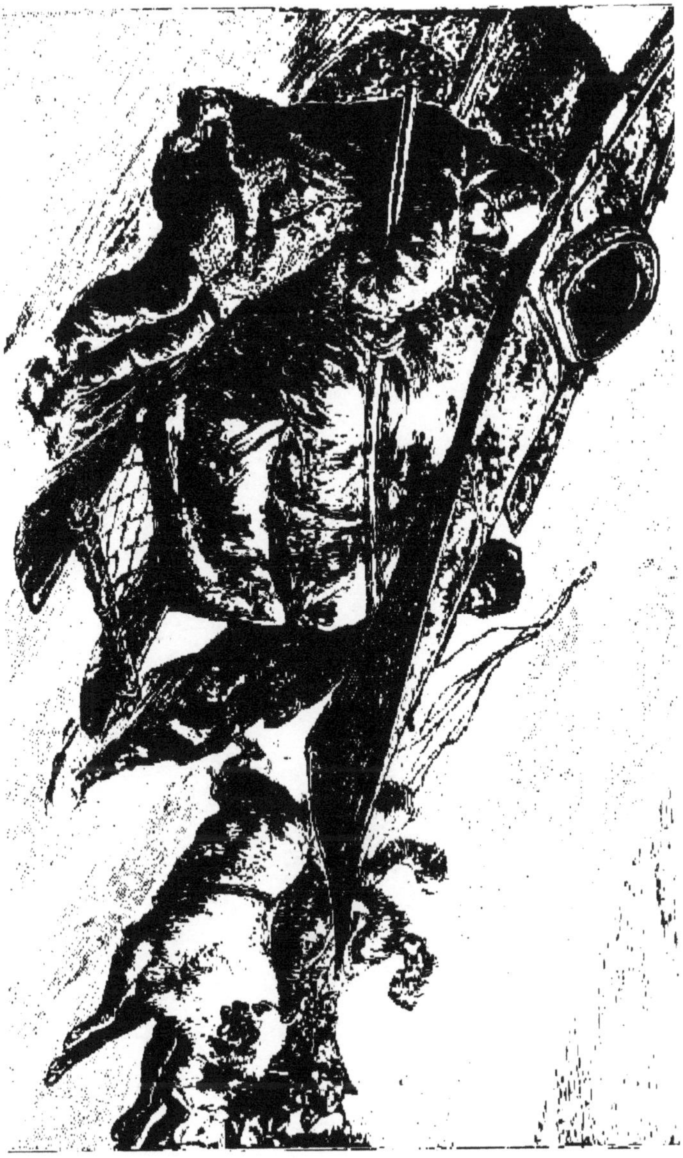

panic, broke their traces, and dashed off, leaving the sledge to descend by its own momentum at a terrific rate, and tasking the efforts of two of the men to keep it from utter wreck.

For upwards of ninety miles Lieutenant Schwatka followed a branch of Back River, along the ice-bound surface of which the sledges moved with comparative celerity, and avoided the rocky ridges which intersected the country. About noon, on May 14th, the travellers came upon a freshly-cut block of snow, turned up on end—an unmistakable indication that natives had quite recently visited the spot; and a little further on, fresh footprints in the snow conducted them to "a cache" of musk-ox meat, and, close by, a deserted igloo. By these signs, Equeesik was able to inform them that they were in the Ooquusik-Sillik country; and as the natives never wander far from the Ooquusik-Sillik, or Back River, this was welcome intelligence to the travellers, who were all excitement at the prospect of speedily meeting them.

Next day their anticipations were realized; the natives appeared. On both sides some distrust was felt. Lieutenant Schwatka and his white men seized their rifles or revolvers; their Eskimos armed themselves with snow-knives and spears. All then advanced towards the igloos; but not a soul was visible. When within about three hundred yards of the native camp, Schwatka's party halted; while Equeesik and Ishnark moved a few paces ahead, and began shouting in the Innuit tongue. Presently one man crawled timidly out of the doorway of an igloo and asked a question, which it is to be presumed was answered satisfactorily; for other natives soon followed, and ranged themselves by his side. Then all of them shouted an invitation to advance, whereupon the white men moved forward with their followers, and conversation between them and the Innuits became general. All the natives carried knives in their hands, which, as weapons, were useless, most of them being simply bits of hoop-iron or of copper, worked down to a blade, and fastened upon long handles of reindeer horn.

From one of these Eskimos, an old man, aged sixty-five or seventy, named Ikinnelikpatolek, Schwatka learned that only once before had he seen white men alive. He was then a little boy, and was fishing in Back River when the strangers came along in a boat —ten of them—and shook hands with him. The leader was called "Tos-ard-e-roak," which, from the

nd, Joe, the interpreter, thought must mean Lieutenant Back. The next white man he saw lay dead in the bunk of a great ship which was frozen in the ice near an island about five miles due west of Grant Point, on Adelaide Peninsula. He and his companions had to walk out about three miles on smooth ice to reach the vessel. His son, he said, a man about thirty-five years old, was then a child, and he pointed to a child of seven or eight years to explain his meaning. About the same time he noticed the tracks of white men on the mainland; at first four, afterwards only three. This was when the spring snows were falling. When his people saw the ship so long deserted, they began to venture on board, and carry off pieces of wood and iron. They found some red cans of fresh meat, with what appeared to be tallow mixed with it. Many had been opened, but four remained untouched. There was no bread. Numerous knives, forks, spoons, pans, cups, and plates were found, and a few books.

In four more marches Schwatka's party reached Back River, and were thus within easy reach of the goal of their enterprise. After examining Montreal Island, they crossed the Dyle Point and Richardson Point peninsulas, and in an inlet west of the latter fell in with a Netchellik encampment. The ceremony of opening communication was similar to that with the Ooquusik-Silliks a few days before; with the exception that instead of remaining in their igloos, the men were drawn up in line-of-battle in front of them, and sent out an old woman to ascertain who the newcomers were and what they wanted. A skilful stratagem; for, had their designs been hostile, and they had killed the old woman, the fighting strength of the Eskimos would not have been reduced, while there would have been one old woman the less to provide for! They carried their bows in their hands, with arrows fixed to the strings; but when the old woman shouted back that the strangers were white men, they laid aside their arms, and received them in a friendly fashion, striking their breasts, and saying, "Many-tume." Joe afterwards said that one of the men wanted a fight "anyhow." It seems that it was their custom to kill the first stranger who came among them after a death in the tribe, and as this was the case with the white men, the amiable Netchellik was anxious to keep up the tradition. At Equeesik's suggestion, however, a gun had been fired as they approached, and probably the knowledge of the effect of the white men's fire-arms protected them from attack.

Next day, they learned from an old man named

Secututuar that he had seen a number of skeletons near the water-line in an inlet about three or four miles to the west of their then camp; also books and papers scattered among the rocks, with knives and forks, spoons, dishes, and cans. There was no sledge, but a boat, which was afterwards broken up and taken away by the natives to be wrought up into wooden implements. On being shown a watch, he said he saw several things like it lying about the shore, which were also collected and broken by the children. Some were silver, and some gold. The bones, he added, would still be there, unless carried off by wolves and foxes.

Further information about the boat place having been received, our explorers equipped one of the sledges and set out to find it. It proved to be about three miles from camp. Though the ground was white with snow, and nothing distinguished it from the coast on either side, they could not but feel the pathetic interest with which the sad fate of Franklin's gallant followers had invested it. To their minds little doubt existed that it marked the farthest point in the direction of Hudson Bay that any one of them had reached. The party was small in number, and, probably, had been thinned down, on "the survival of the fittest" principle, to the few hardiest, whose anticipation of rescue or hope of escape from a melancholy death had not failed them under all their sufferings, so long as they kept the frozen mainland in view. It probably seemed to them that if they could but set foot upon its shore they would be comparatively safe. Yet the bravest hearts must have sunk—and brave hearts were doubtlessly among them—when they surveyed the awful desolation of the country. No more striking picture of utter abandonment does the whole world present. The land is barren and low; so low, that its level can scarcely be distinguished from the sea when a mantle of snow lies heavily upon both. Neither tree nor bush, nor flower nor wood, scarcely a hill visible; nothing to relieve the oppressive monotony of the scene. No living thing, no sign of life anywhere visible, though the eye ranges uninterruptedly over a vast extent of territory. Even a wolf prowling to and fro would be a relief in the absolute silence and solitude that surround and overwhelm the explorer.

Such were the reflections present to the minds of our adventurers as they looked around but saw no traces of the lost Englishmen. Had they known at the time what they learned a few days later, the place would have acquired an additional interest as the spot where the records of the expedition, which had been brought thus far with infinite toil and care, had been irrecoverably lost. They marked the site carefully, with a view to a thorough investigation when the snow was off the ground, and then returned to camp.

Among the natives in the neighbourhood was a Netchellik woman, named Ahlangyah, about fifty-five years old. She proved to be one of a party who had met some of the survivors of the ill-fated ships in Washington Bay. She indicated the eastern coast of the bay as the spot where she, in company with her husband and two other men and their wives, had seen, many years ago, ten white men dragging a sledge with a boat on it. The sledge was on the ice, and separated from the Innuits by a broad fissure. The women went on shore, and the men awaited the white strangers at the crack in the ice. Five of the white men put up a tent on the shore; the five others remained in the boat. The Innuits erected a tent near the white men, and the two parties remained together for five days. During this time the Innuits killed a number of seals on the ice, which they gave to the white men. Ahlangyah said that her husband was presented by the strangers with a chopping-knife. At the end of five days all started for Adelaide Peninsula, fearing that, if they longer delayed, the ice being very rotten, they would not be able to cross; and they travelled at night when the sun was low, because the ice would then be a little frozen. The white men followed: but as they dragged their heavy sledge and boat, they could not move as rapidly as the Innuits, who halted and waited for them at Gladman Point. The Innuits, on account of the rotten condition of the ice, could not cross to the mainland, and remained in King William Land all the summer. The white men they never saw again, though they waited at Gladman Point, fishing in the neighbouring lakes, going to and fro between the shore and lakes nearly all the summer, and finally pushing across to the eastern shore.

The white men, said Ahlangyah, were without fur clothing; some of them were very thin, and their mouths were hard and dry and black. When asked if she remembered the names of any of the white men, she said one of them was called "Agloocar" and another "Toolooah." As these are common Eskimo names, we must suppose that the names she heard given to the white men resembled them in sound, and were thus impressed upon her memory. Another of the strangers was called "Ook-took" (doctor). "Toolooah" was a little older than the others, and had a large black beard, mixed with gray. He was bigger than any of the others—"a big, broad man." "Agloocar" was smaller, and had a brown beard about four or five inches long. "Ook-took" was a short man, with a big stomach, and a red beard about the size of "Agloocar's."

Ahlangyah concluded her statement by saying that, in the following spring, when the ground was almost clear of snow, she saw a tent standing on the shore at the head of Terror Bay. There were dead bodies in the tent, and outside lay some covered over with sand. There was no flesh on them, nothing but the bones and clothes. She saw nothing to indicate that they had belonged to the party she met before. The bones had the cords or sinews still attached to them. Outside were one or two graves, which the natives did not at that time open. Numerous articles were lying around, such as knives, forks, spoons, watches, many books, clothing, and blankets.

When she had finished her story, "we gave her," says one of Schwatka's party, "some needles, spoons, a tin pan, and other articles, that well repaid her for the trouble she had taken. Here was a woman who had actually seen the poor, starving explorers, and her story was replete with interest for us. Every word she uttered seemed fraught with the dread tragedy; and she appeared to share our interest, for her face was full of expression. At times it was saddened with the recital of the piteous condition of the white men, and tears filled her eyes as she recalled the sad scene at the tent place where so many had perished and their bodies become food for wild beasts.

It would seem that the party who perished in the inlet belonged to the party she met on King William Land. She and her friends could not get across Simpson Strait, while the white men kept on over the rotten ice— probably at last compelled to take to their boats, and then, at the mercy of the wind and ice, after losing others of their number near Pfeffer River and Todd Islands, had drifted into the inlet where the dead bodies were found with the boat. How long it took them to reach this place will probably never be known, but there is little doubt that they were in a desperate condition; in fact, as we subsequently learned from other witnesses, there were almost unmistakable evidences of their having been compelled to resort to cannibalism, until at last they absolutely starved to death at this point. At least all but one, whose remains were found, during the summer after our visit here, about five miles further inland."

Our explorers secured a valuable relic here in the sledge seen by Sir Leopold M'Clintock in Erebus Bay, which at that time carried a boat with several skeletons inside it. After passing into the hands of the Innuits, it was frequently cut down. It was originally seven feet longer, while the runners were about two inches higher and twice as far apart.

CHAPTER II.

THE STORIES OF THE NATIVES.

ON the evening of the 4th of June our explorers met a young man named Adlekok, who, during the previous summer, had found a new cairn erected by white men near Pfeffer River, which had never been seen by any other Innuits. Near it were three graves, and a tent place in which he found a pair of wire gauze "snow-goggles:" these our travellers purchased of him. Acting on this information, Lieutenant Schwatka and Mr. Gilder took a light sledge, and with Toolooah as driver and Adlekok as guide, hastened to the spot. They carried one day's rations with them, in case they should be detained overnight; and started with a head wind in their teeth, and a storm lowering around that obstructed the view except in the immediate vicinity of the sledge. Their guide, however, drove them through a trackless waste of smooth ice for a distance of over twenty-five miles without deviation from the direct line, though he had neither sun nor landmarks to steer by. Forward, forward, with the unerring instinct of the sleuth-hound, until they struck the land on the western bank of Pfeffer River. On arriving at the cairn they at once perceived that it was undoubtedly what Adlekok had called it, "a white man's cairn." Before proceeding to pull it to pieces, they examined it carefully, and found scratched on a clay-stone, with the point of a sharp instrument, the following inscription:—

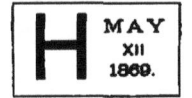

> H MAY XII 1869.

And on the opposite side:—

> ETERNAL HONOUR TO THE DISCOVERERS OF
> THE NORTH WE...

Then they knew it to be the cairn which their countryman Captain Hall had raised over the bones of two of Franklin's men, whose remains he speaks of having found there.

From a native named Ogzenekjenwoek, an *aruketko*, or "medicine-man," who was a lad of about twelve years old when he first visited "the boat place," and from his mother, some interesting, if painful, particulars were obtained.

It appears that they never met with any of Franklin's men alive, but saw four skeletons on the mainland, and two on an adjacent island—an island on the southern coast in long. 95° W. At neither place were any graves. They found at the boat place a tin box, the contents of which were printed books, each about two feet long and a foot wide, and among them what was probably the needle of a compass or other magnetic instrument, for they said that when it touched iron it stuck fast. Outside the boat were skulls; the exact number they could not remember, but more than four. They also found a quantity of bones from legs and arms which appeared to have been sawed off. Inside the boat was a box filled with bones, the box being about the same size as the one with books in it; and from their appearance the Innuits concluded "that the white men had been eating each other." What little flesh still adhered to the bones was very fresh; one body was fully covered. The hair was light, and the body looked like that of a tall man. Ogzenekjenwoek saw a number of wire "snow-goggles," and alongside the body with flesh on it was a pair of gold spectacles. He discovered more than one or two pairs of such spectacles, but had forgotten how many. When asked how long the bodies appeared to have been dead, he replied that they had probably died during the previous winter.

In the boat he saw canvas and four sticks (that is, either a tent or a sail), and several open-faced watches, some of which were gold, but most silver. These were given to the children to play with, but had been broken up and lost. One body, that with flesh on, wore a gold chain fastened to gold ear-rings, and a gold hunting-case watch attached to the chain, and hanging down about the waist. The Eskimo added that when he pulled the chain, it pulled the head up by the ears. This body had also a gold ring on the ring-finger of the right hand. In reference to this statement, the American chronicler of Schwatka's expedition remarks that the chain may in some way have become attached to the ears, or, ridiculous as the story sounds, there may have been some eccentric person in the party who wore his watch in that way; and if such should prove to be the case, this would certainly identify him beyond doubt. But we believe no such identification has taken place.

SUPPOSED CANNIBALISM.

The Eskimo's reason for thinking that the survivors of Franklin's expedition had resorted to cannibalism was, because the bones had been cut with a knife or a saw. A big saw and a small saw were found in the boat; also a large red tin can of smoking tobacco and some pipes. There was no cairn at the place. The bones, he said, were now covered up with sand and sea-weed, as they were lying just at high-water mark.*

It seems not improbable that the skeletons found at this place were the remains of some of the party who were seen by Ahlangyah and her friends in Washington Bay. The gold watches are a testimony that there were officers in the party. The five men

* Admiral Richards, in a letter to the *Times* (October 20, 1880), speaks of the assertion that Franklin's men in their last extremity resorted to cannibalism as without "one tittle of foundation;" and it will be seen that the American writers give absolutely no valid reasons in support of it. The Eskimo based his conviction on the fact that some of the limbs had been removed as if by a saw. Supposing this to be the case, the natives were probably the operators. "The intercourse between the natives and such of Franklin's men as they met with is surrounded with circumstances of grave suspicion as gathered from themselves, and this suspicion derives strength from various circumstances related on Schwatka's journey. Certainly he and his party appear to have had little confidence in the tribes they met with in the neighbourhood of the Great Fish River; and if there was any foul play towards the retreating parties of Franklin's ships, it would manifestly be to the interest of the natives to divert suspicion from themselves by any means in their power." Admiral Richards goes on to point out that the crews of the *Erebus* and the *Terror*, when they abandoned their ships, were doubtless for the most part suffering from exhaustion and scurvy; death had been

who had a tent on shore were perhaps officers. We may surmise that the books found in the tin box were the more important records of the expedition, and in charge of the chief surviving officers. It is unlikely that men reduced to dire extremity, and compelled to drag everything by land, would burden themselves with miscellaneous reading matter. Judging from the relics obtained, the boat must have been a heavy one and copper-bottomed; for most of the kettles found in use among the Netchelliks were made of sheet copper, which came, they said, from this and the other boats in Erebus Bay. But as it was an absolute necessity, the unfortunate castaways could not abandon it. During the year and a half

staring them in the face for months. They started to undertake a journey which men in strong health and under the most "favourable circumstances might well have shrunk from as hopeless. It was, in fact, a forlorn hope. The greater part of them probably died from exhaustion and disease long before they had got one hundred miles from their ships, and found their graves beneath the ice when it melted in summer, or on the beach of King William Land. It may be assumed that no more than half-a dozen out of the whole crews ever reached the entrance of the Great Fish River. We need not call in starvation to our aid. I fully believe that by far the greater portion perished long before their provisions were consumed. The only thing that would have restored men to convalescence in their condition would have been nursing and the comforts of hospital treatment, not a resort to human flesh. The thing appears so monstrous to me that I am at a loss to conceive how it can have been suggested. Death would have had no terror for men in their position. It may perhaps be thought that I am dealing in probabilities; but I will gladly be judged by any officer who has ever served in the Arctic regions as to the soundness of my views."

that the *Erebus* and the *Terror* were frozen fast in Victoria Strait, the officers, we may assume, surveyed with care the adjacent shores, and undoubtedly made many highly important observations. This would more particularly be the case with their magnetic observations, as they were close to the magnetic pole. Schwatka's party discovered some tall and very conspicuous cairns near Cape Felix, which were without records, and had apparently been erected as points of observation from the ships. As their bitter experiences of distress and exhaustion began after they abandoned their vessels, it is fair to conclude that their time had, up to this epoch, been occupied in scientific work, and that their records of it were contained in the tin box which the Netchelliks found and unhappily destroyed.

Our explorers, on the 17th of June, started for Cape Felix. Their course was a little to the west of north, and at night they encamped at the head of Washington Bay. Here they left the salt-water ice, and fared across the land, keeping in the same direction, with the view of striking Collinson Inlet near its head. After ten days' travel, however, they came out, owing to an error on the Admiralty charts, upon Erebus Bay. The land travel was very heavy and tedious, owing to the softening condition of the snow, and to the lakes being covered with water some six to eight inches deep. In the morning the slight crust on the snow formed during the night would break through at nearly every step, while during the rest of the day the men simply waded through slush or water.

They found the salt-water ice also in a bad condition for travelling. It was very old ice, and as "hummocky" as it was possible for ice to be. They usually kept near the coast, where sledging was comparatively easy; but one day they ventured across the hummocks, in order to avoid a long circuit, and came to great grief. The winter winds had piled up the autumn snows around and among the hummocks, filling in the interstices so that if the snow had been frozen the sledging would not have been so very difficult; but the sun's rays had already poured upon it, day and night, for so long a period that the snow was soft, and nearly every step broke through it. Sometimes the travellers sank to their waists, and then their legs would dangle in slush and water and no bottom be found. Sometimes the sledge plunged so deeply that, light as was its load, they could not extricate it; and when the party gathered around to help them, they could get only an occasional foothold, perhaps by kneeling on a hummock, or holding on with one hand while they tugged lustily with the other. Even the dogs pulled to no profit. Some would be floundering in the slush and water, while others scrambled over the broken ice; yet such was the craft of the Innuit dog-driver, that in spite of every obstacle they made a ten miles' march.

Toolooah was not only a dog-driver of exceptional address, but a mighty hunter, a Nimrod of the Innuit race. When the weather was unfavourable for hunting, and the party without food, the Innuits were wont to say, "Ma-muk-poo-now" (No good), and sit down to wait until the weather bettered. In such an emergency, however, Toolooah would rise, gird up his loins, and sally forth in pursuit of game. The others would perhaps go forth, and, for a short time, look around for game also, returning empty-handed; but Toolooah kept up his quest until midnight. On one occasion the adventurers were all without food, and moving into a part of the country which they knew to be too thinly stocked with game. Forth fared the hunters through the snow-drifts. The snow was falling heavily, and the sole chance of seeing reindeer lay in their stumbling upon them unobserved by the accident of approaching them toward the wind. All but Toolooah returned about noon, discouraged, without having sighted game. Toolooah, the mighty hunter, however, was five hours later; and then he came in for the dogs to fetch three reindeer which he had killed a few miles north of the camp.

The ten-mile march through Erebus Bay occupied fifteen hours, and right glad were the wayfarers when they reached the shore, some distance below Franklin Point. There they encamped, and then they rested on the day following—a day marked by a pathetic incident, for in the course of it Mr. Gilder shot two of an apparently new species of snipe to preserve their skins for a zoological museum. "One of them," he says, "was distinguished by a sweet simple song, somewhat similar to that of the lark, its silvery tones gushing forth as if in perfect ecstasy of enjoyment of air and sunshine, at the same time rising and poising itself upon its wings. It seemed almost inhuman to kill the sweet little songster, particularly as it was the only creature I saw in the Arctic world that uttered a pleasant note. All other sounds were such as the scream of the hawk and the gull, the quack of the duck, the yell of the wolf, the 'ooff! ooff!' of the walrus, or the bark of the seal: all harsh and unmelodious, save the tones of this sweet little singer.

Nothing but starvation or scientific research could justify the slaughter of one of these innocents. I believe I shut my eyes when I pulled the trigger of my gun, and I know my heart gave a regretful thump when I heard the thud of its poor, bleeding body upon the ground."

After passing Franklin Point, the four white men of the party kept upon the land near the coast-line, while the Innuits, with the sledge, followed along the shore ice. Before reaching Collinson Inlet, they fell in with the graves of two white men. The upper part of a skull was lying near one of them, with some other bones, which were decently reinterred. Henry and Frank afterwards, at the distance of a mile and a half from their camp, came upon the camp made by Captain Crozier with all his crews after abandoning the two discovery vessels. There were several cooking-stoves, with their accompanying copper kettles, besides clothing, blankets, canvas, iron and brass implements, and an open grave. This contained a quantity of blue cloth, part of which seemed to have been a heavy overcoat, and had probably been used to wrap around the body. A huge quantity of canvas was also found in and about the grave, with coarse stitching through it and the cloth, as if the body had been

DISCOVERY OF LIEUTENANT IRVING'S GRAVE. *Page 50.*

encased for burial at sea. Several gilt buttons lay among the rotting cloth and mould in the bottom of the grave, and a lens, apparently the object-glass of a marine telescope. Upon one of the stones at the foot of the grave Henry found a medal thickly covered with grime. It was of silver, two and a half inches in diameter, with a bas-relief portrait of George IV., encircled by the words—

> GEORGIUS IIII. D.G. BRITANNIARUM
> REX. 1820.

on the obverse; and on the reverse a laurel wreath surrounded by—

> SECOND MATHEMATICAL PRIZE,
> ROYAL NAVAL COLLEGE

and enclosing the words—

> AWARDED TO JOHN IRVING.
> MIDSUMMER, 1830.

This relic at once identified the grave as that of Lieutenant John Irving, third officer of the *Terror*. A figured silk pocket-handkerchief, neatly folded, the colours and pattern of which were in a remarkable state of preservation, was placed under the head. Only the skull and a few other bones were found in or near the grave.

Lieutenant Irving's remains were carefully transported to New York, and thence sent back to Edinburgh, his native city. There they were honoured with a public funeral on the occasion of their interment in Dean Cemetery, Friday, the 7th of January 1881. Each of the regiments in the Edinburgh garrison was represented by a party of twenty-eight men (the 21st Hussars, the Royal Artillery, and the 71st Highlanders), and H.M.S. *Warden* furnished a contingent of one hundred and fifty marines and sailors. The procession was also accompanied by the band and pipers of the 71st Regiment; and a great concourse of sight-seers thronged the entire route from the starting-point in Great King Street to the cemetery. The coffin was of solid oak, and on the lid was a brass plate, simply inscribed, "John Irving, Lieutenant R.N. Born 1815; died 1848–9." The chief naval and military authorities were present, and many of the leading citizens of Edinburgh; and nothing was left undone that could add to the dignity and impressiveness of the scene. Lieutenant Irving, we may add, was the fourth son of the late Mr. John Irving, W.S., of Edinburgh, a schoolfellow and friend of Sir Walter Scott. Born in 1815, he entered the navy in 1828; afterwards spent a few years as a sheep-farmer in Australia; obtained his lieutenant's commission in 1843; and was appointed to the *Terror* in 1845.

The day after this discovery, Lieutenant Schwatka moved his camp to the vicinity of the dead officer's last resting-place, and spent two days in searching round about, but ineffectually at that time, as the snow still covered the ground. But when they returned there from Cape Felix, on the 11th of July, they found the snow nearly gone and the ponds near the shore almost all dried up. Accordingly they renewed their search, and with more success. Among the various articles that rewarded their labour was a brush with the name " H. Wilks" cut in the side, a two-gallon stone jug stamped "R. Wheatly, wine and spirit merchant, Greenhithe, Kent," several tin cans, a pickle bottle, and a canvas pulling strap, a sledge harness marked with a stencil plate " T 11," showing it to have belonged to the *Terror*.

On their second visit, Toolooah's wife discovered in a pile of stones a piece of paper which, *mirabile dictu*, had weathered the Arctic storms of thirty years. It proved to be a copy of the Crozier record found by Lieutenant Hobson of the M'Clintock expedition, and was in the handwriting of Sir Leopold M'Clintock. The document was written with a lead pencil on notepaper, and was partially illegible from exposure. It was literally as follows:—

"*May 7, 1859.*
"Lat. 69° 38′ N., long. 98° 41′ W.

"This cairn was found yesterday by a party from Lady Franklin's discovery yacht *Fox*, now wintering in Bellot Strait......a notice of which the following is......removed:—

"'*28th May 1847.*

"'H.M. ships *Erebus* and *Terror* wintered in the ice in lat. 70° 05′ N., long. 98° 23′ W., having wintered at Beechy Island in lat. 74° 43′ 28″ N., long. 91° 39′ 15″ W., after having ascended Wellington Channel to lat. 77°, and returned by the west side of Cornwallis Island.

"'Sir John Franklin commanding the expedition. All well. A party of two officers and six men left the ships on Monday, the 24th May.

"'Graham Gore.
"'Charles F. Des V......'

" ......into a......printed form, which was a request in six languages that if picked up it might be forwarded to the British Admiralty."

Round the margin of this paper was—

"'*The 25th April 1848.*

"'H.M. ships *Terror* and *Erebus* were deserted on the 22nd April......opens to the N.N.Wd. of this, having been beset since 12th Sept. 1846. The officers and crews, consisting of 105 souls, under the command of Captain F. M. Crozier, landed here in lat. 69° 37′ 42″ N., long. 98° 41′ W.

"'This paper was found by Lieutenant Irving under the cairn supposed to have been built by Sir James Ross in 1831, four miles to the northward, where it had been deposited by the late Commander Gore in June 1847. Sir James Ross's pillar, however, has not been found ...... the paper has been transferred......this position, which......was erected.

"'Sir John Franklin died on the 7th of June 1847, and the total loss by deaths in the expedition has been......officers and fifteen men.

"'F. M. Crozier,
Captain and Senior Officer.
"'James Fitzjames,
Captain H.M.S. Erebus.
"'And start to-morrow for Back's Fish River.'

"At this cairn, which we reached......noon yesterday; the last cairn appears to have made a selection of your (?) for travelling—leaving all that was superfluous strewn about its vicinity. I remained at this spot until nearly noon of to-day, searching for relics, etc. No other papers......been found.

"It is my intention to follow the land to the S.W., in quest of the wreck of a ship said by the Esquimaux to be on the beach. Three other cairns have been found between this and Cape Felix......They contain no infor......about it.

"WILLIAM R. HOBSON,
"*Lieutenant in charge of party.*"

"This paper is a copy of a record left here by Captain Crozier when retreating with the crews of the *Erebus* and *Terror* to the Great Fish River: the information of its discovery by Lieut. W. R. Hobson is intended for me. As the natives appear to have pulled down a cairn erected here in 1831, I purpose burying a record at ten feet due north from the centre of this cairn, and at one foot below the surface.

"F. L. M'CLINTOCK, *Capt. R.N.*"

Lieutenant Schwatka at once employed his men to

dig up the record supposed to have been buried by Captain M'Clintock; but though they dug a deep trench four feet wide from the centre of the cairn, due north, for a distance of twenty feet, nothing was found; and hence it was inferred either that Captain M'Clintock had forgotten to deposit the record, or that changes in the surface of the ground had revealed it—in which case it may have been stolen by the Innuits, who cannot be expected to possess any very elevated ideas of the sanctity of property, or washed into the sea.

The conclusion at which our adventurers arrived was, that on abandoning their vessels the crews landed at this historic spot, having carried with them nothing more than was necessary for their sledge journey. When, after a wearisome and exhausting effort, they reached the southern coast of King William Land, their condition was so pitiful that a small party was hastily sent back for provisions. The Ookjoolik, who saw the ship that sank off Grant Point, has proved that even then there was a small quantity of stores on board. In charge of this return party was probably Lieutenant Irving, and it seems that he died after reaching the camp. We may assume that the white men who, according to the Ookjooliks, drifted with the ship to the island off Grant Point, also belonged to this party, and, with the true sailor's instinct, preferred to stick to the ship rather than crawl back to the famishing party which they had left, with scarcely any better prospects, on the south coast. From the appearances of the boat place at Erebus Bay, it may be conjectured that the hapless vessel floated ashore after the *débâcle* of the ice, having previously been deserted by all who were able to walk. That skeletons were discovered in the boat by those who saw it before it was gradually destroyed, as well as by Schwatka's party, is a proof, we fear, that at the time the whole company were reduced to an extremity; otherwise we may be sure that the helpless would never have been forsaken.

We need not pursue this line of speculation further. An impenetrable shroud of mystery has for ever descended upon the latest struggles and sufferings of Franklin's ill-fated followers. We can but think of them as wan and haggard—skeletons rather than men—dragging their slow steps across the rough and difficult ice; growing fainter, feebler every hour; and at last, one by one, succumbing to the fatal influence of the Arctic cold, and dropping on the frozen snow, to rise no more. No sorrowing wife or mother received their last sigh; alone, in that fearful Northern silence, they passed away!

Lieutenant Schwatka's party left Irving Bay on the 30th of June, and on the 3rd of July reached Cape Felix. No traces of the Franklin expedition were seen until they reached their place of encampment. Every day developed for them new pains and penalties in walking; revealed fresh horrors in the route they pursued. Either they waded through the shallow lakes, or torrents, which, being frozen at the bottom, were exceedingly treacherous to the feet; or else, with their sealskin boots rendered soft by constant immersion, they painfully plodded over sharp claystones set firmly in the ground, with the edges pointing up, or lying flat and slippery as they stepped upon them, and betraying the unwary foot into a crevice with a shock that threatened to wrench it from the body. These are but a few of the disagreeabilities of travel in King William Land; yet, with courageous pertinacity, our wayfarers accomplished about ten miles a day, and made as complete an investigation on all sides as was possible. They began to experience some privation from want of "civilized food." Lieutenant Schwatka, with his double-barrelled shot-gun, killed ducks and geese very freely, and Mr. Gilder's rifle brought down an occasional reindeer. In time they were reduced to an exclusively meat diet, and, as the flesh was eaten almost as soon as killed, they all suffered more or less from diarrhœa. Nor did they obtain any other food until nine months later, when they reached the ship *George and Mary* at Marble Island, except a few pounds of raw starch, which they had left at Cape Herschel on starting for Cape Felix in the previous June. But against physical discomfort might fairly be set the pleasure they derived from the landscape, which, in the warm summer glow, was not without a weird beauty of its own.

Lieutenant Schwatka left Cape Felix on the 7th of July, reluctantly satisfied that Sir John Franklin had not been buried in that neighbourhood. His search had been thorough and complete, and had greatly engaged the interest of the Innuits. Since Toolooah's discovery of the inscription scratched on a clay-stone by Captain Hall he had been specially vigilant. Often when out hunting, he came upon a stone near a demolished cairn, or in some conspicuous place, and if it had marks upon its surface which he supposed to be writing, he invariably brought it into camp, though compelled, perhaps, to carry it a long distance,

VIEW IN SUMMER, KING WILLIAM LAND.

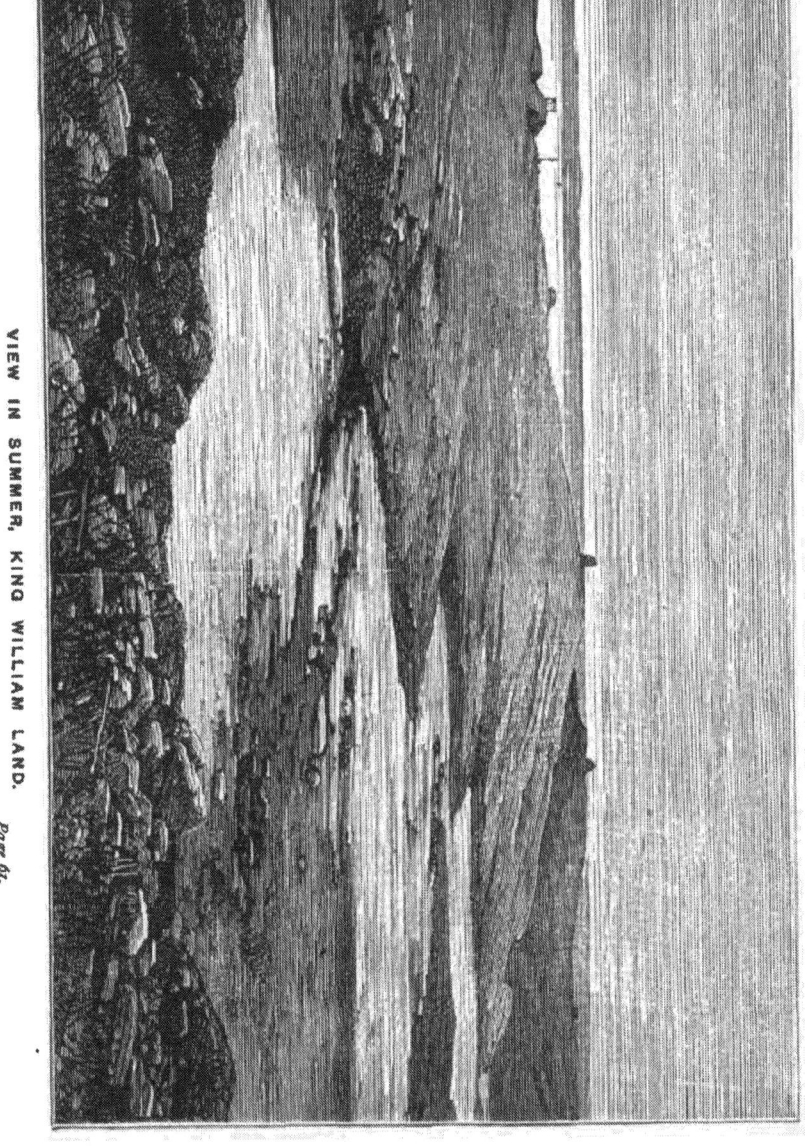

Page 61.

in addition to a load of meat. He was as "untiring" to aid them in their search as in securing food supplies, and invariably displayed in all his actions a degree of intelligence "wholly foreign to Innuit character."

CHAPTER III.

RETRACING THEIR STEPS.

HAVING accomplished the task they had undertaken; having searched King William Land thoroughly, and carefully reburied the remains of Franklin's ill-fated followers, they remained on the island until the ice—which had broken up on the 24th of July, with its usual picturesque effects—was again sufficiently strong to carry them back to the mainland; and then, on the 8th of November, they recrossed Simpson Strait, coasted Adelaide Peninsula on the west, and selected a track for their homeward journey about sixty miles westward of their outward route. On the 12th they reached a native camp near the mouth of Sherman Inlet, having been delayed by fogs and snow-showers and the heavily-loaded sledges. The Eskimos, among whom were some they had met during the spring, received them with a great shout of "Many-tu-me!"

their usual cry of welcome. An igloo was speedily raised; and during the time the adventurers remained with them their solicitude for their comfort was incessant. "It seemed as if some one were on the roof of our igloo all the time patching up holes; and they changed the direction of the doorway every time the wind changed, and that kept them busy all the time."

Resuming their march, they kept to the south-east for several days, travelling about forty-five miles. The sun was so low now that they had either sunrise or sunset so long as it was above the horizon. At noon it was not more than four degrees high. They were gradually moving southward, or this would have been all their light during the day-time. As a matter of course, for several days before they left Back River, the sun showed only its diameter above the coast-side hills, and, after a brief exhibition of its luminous sphere, left them to work in the long twilight, which was succeeded by the longer darkness. They could travel but slowly when the days were so short, especially as the sledges carried a heavy burden and the dogs were but half-fed. The softness of the snow on the land, where as yet it was not thoroughly packed, and the minute particles of ice that froze on its surface, were also obstacles. In many places the river and lakes were absolutely free from snow, and the bare ice took off the ice from the sledge-runners as if it were rock. This mattered not at all while the river-ice was bare,—the sledges slipped along merrily, and the dogs ran; but so joyful a state of things seldom lasted for more than half a mile, when the sledges again came upon the snow, and a more laborious drag was the consequence. We have spoken of the dogs as half-fed: well, on two occasions there was an interval of *eight* days between their meals. That they could work, or even live, seemed little short of a miracle; and it may be admitted, we think, that "the Eskimo dog will do more work with less food than any draught animal existing."

On the night of the 20th, Lieutenant Schwatka observed a meridian culmination of the moon, which showed that they were in lat. 67° 32′ 42″ N., only three miles from their reckoning. Difficult was it to take astronomical observations with a sextant in a temperature 38° below zero, or 70° below the freezing-point, as it was on that very night. To sit still for any length of time in such weather was far from agreeable! A film of ice formed on the surface of the kerosene oil which was used for an artificial horizon, and had to be constantly removed by the warm breath of an assistant. The breath of the observer froze on the sextant glasses, which had to be cleaned with the fingers at the cost of blistering them. These, we are told, are *some* of the obstacles to determining one's position astronomically in an Arctic winter. The mean temperature for November was $-23°\ 3'$, and the minimum, as noted, $-49°$.

The 5th of December found them near the Dangerous Rapids on Back River, which they proceeded to descend to its point of confluence with Chesterfield Inlet. They experienced no little suffering on their journey, owing to the bare ice in the neighbourhood of the open water rapids, and the intense cold which filled the air with minute particles of ice from the freezing of the steam of the open water. These atoms, it is added, fell upon the hard snow, which otherwise would have been good sledging, and, remaining separated from each other, could be brushed up like sand, and, indeed, were nearly as hard as sand, so that to drag the sledges along was almost impossible. The thermometer frequently registered 50° and 60° below zero, while the wayfarers moved with a strong wind blowing directly in their faces. At this time they were living wholly upon reindeer meat. The dogs had begun to feel the combined effects of hard work, cold weather, and low diet, and before the end of December they had lost a couple, while, in all, seven-and-twenty perished before the party reached Depot Island.

On the 28th of December, in order to shorten the journey, Lieutenant Schwatka left the river and struck across country for Depot Island. The thermometer reached the lowest point observed during the journey on the 3rd of January 1880: in the morning, −70°; at noon, −69°; and at five P.M., −71°. January proved an exceedingly stormy month, and there were only eleven days out of the thirty-one on which travelling was possible, so that not more than ninety-one miles were accomplished. The party followed up musk-ox tracks for about twenty-five miles, but desisted on finding that wolves were ahead of them and had already scared the game away. The country swarmed with reindeer, so that on every hillside the breath of the herds rose like clouds of steam. A herd that was terrified by the dogs, which were pursuing the musk-ox tracks, sped away in every direction, so that it looked as if a host of locomotives had been let loose, the smoke issuing from their nostrils in great puffs as they ran and streaming like meteors behind them. When the sledges were moving on a clear cold day, their relative positions, however far they might be apart, were easily known. Occasionally, for the advantage of hunting over a wider area of country, their igloos were pitched at a distance of ten miles apart; and at that distance the condensed breath of the dogs and people could be distinctly seen and their location determined.

Almost every day now the travellers lost one of their dogs. Of reindeer meat the supply was ample; but it was usually frozen, and in that state has but small nourishing quality in weather when fat and warming food are specially needful. Many of the dogs would have been saved if to each a seal's skin full of blubber could have been allowed weekly; but there was none to spare; it had to be reserved for lighting the igloos at night. To expend it for culinary or heating purposes was impossible. All the meals were served up cold; a pleasant change at an English picnic, but a disagreeable necessity in a Polar land and in mid-winter! The frozen meat was so solid that it had to be sawed, and then broken up into lumps of a convenient size, which, when first put into the mouth, were hard as stones; or cooked with moss gathered from the hillsides, after the snow had been beaten off it with a stick. It is true that meat will freeze in a temperature a little below 32°; but it is even in that case very different in condition to what it is when frozen at from 50° to 70° below zero! For then every piece of meat one puts in one's mouth must first be breathed upon to thaw the surface, or it will stick to one's tongue and one's lips, and the sides of one's mouth like red-hot iron, and with results not less exquisitely painful! The luxury of a cooked meal was possible to our adventurers only on the days when they sojourned in camp, as it took nearly four hours to gather the moss and cook the viands.

Wolves were now almost as numerous as reindeer, and would frequently prowl about the igloos. Having killed and devoured four of Equeesik's dogs, and attacked him when he emerged from the igloo to drive them off, he resolved upon revenge. Two of his assailants he killed with his rifles; two others by a contrivance as diabolical as Orsini's or Fieschi's "infernal machine." He set two keenly-sharpened knife-blades in the ice, and covered them with blood, which the wolves licked, and in the process sliced or gashed their tongues. The cold prevented them from feeling the wounds at the time, and their own warm blood tempted them to continue, until their tongues were so scarified that death became inevitable. He also prepared some pills, by rolling up long strings of whalebone bound with sinew and hiding them in meat. When frozen, the bolus held together until it had passed into the animal's intestines; then, the meat having thawed and the sinew digested, the whalebone would expand, and inflict a horrible death. Such treatment as this may be considered bad enough even for wolves!

When Toolooah was out hunting on the 23rd of February, he was attacked by a pack of about twenty wolves. He leaped upon a big rock, which they soon surrounded, and there he fought the ferocious beasts off with the butt of his gun until he could make sure of his aim; then he killed one, and while the others fought over and devoured the carcass, made the best of his way back to camp. A more fortunate escape is scarcely upon record.

On the 4th day of March the party arrived at Depot Island, after an absence of something more than eleven months, having traversed upwards of three thousand miles of country. "Comment on this remarkable undertaking," says Admiral Richards, "seems superfluous. So far as I know it stands unrivalled in the annals of Arctic, or, indeed, of any other enterprise of modern times, and one scarcely knows which to admire most—the boldness and audacity of its conception, or the unswerving devotion and perseverance which brought it to a successful conclusion."

At Depot Island they were received by the natives, whose friendship they had secured on their first visit to the spot. "About noon," says Gilder, "we were within four or five miles, and saw some natives on the ice in the dim distance. Then all was excitement in our party, and it increased as the distance diminished. I never expected to feel so agitated myself as I did when I found myself running and shouting with the natives. Toolooah fired a signal-gun, then jumped on the sledge and waved a deerskin, which had been agreed between him and Armow as announcing our identity on our return. At last the sledge drew near enough to recognize Armow, who was lashing up to us ahead of the others. When they halted he grasped Lieutenant Schwatka by the hand, and shook it long and heartily, saying, 'Ma-muk-poo am-a-suet suk-o' (Plenty good to see); and then he came to me, and I noticed, as he held my hand, that the tears, warm from his dear old heart, were coursing down his cheeks. I was moved, as I scarcely anticipated, at the tenderness and earnest warmth of our reception."

Lieutenant Schwatka had expected to find either ships wintering at Depot Island, or ample supplies of provisions, which Captain Barry, of the whaling ship already mentioned, had promised to leave in charge of Armow the Eskimo. In both expectations he was disappointed; but hearing that a vessel lay at Marble Island, farther to the southward, he proceeded thither as soon as the weather permitted. Meanwhile, the whole community suffered severe privations, being reduced to live upon walrus hide, and of this partaking only once in the twenty-four hours. The privation killed one of the Eskimo women—" Cockeye," the wife of Te-wort, or "Papa;" the funeral ceremonies in whose honour were extended over four days. But hers was the only fatal case. The remainder of the party arrived in safety at Marble Island, where they found a whaling vessel, and obtained abundant supplies.

CHAPTER IV.

SEAL AND WALRUS HUNTING.

MR. GILDER'S narrative of the expedition contains some interesting illustrations of Arctic customs and Eskimo life. The writer describes the skill and assiduity of the Eskimos in fishing, of which he had visible proof at Salmon Creek, near Camp Daly; and lays great stress on the usefulness of the seal, which furnishes the Eskimo not only with food and clothing, but with light and warmth. Its skin is made into dogs' harness and traces, whip-lashes, boots and shoes, gun-covers, water-pails, bags for the storing of oil and blubber, and tent coverings. Sealskin bags, inflated and attached to walrus-lines, are used in hunting walrus and whales; moreover, in summer the Eskimo lives in a tent made of sealskin. A single tent, or "tu-pié," as it is called, is composed of from five to ten skins, which are split; that is, the outer integument is removed and dried

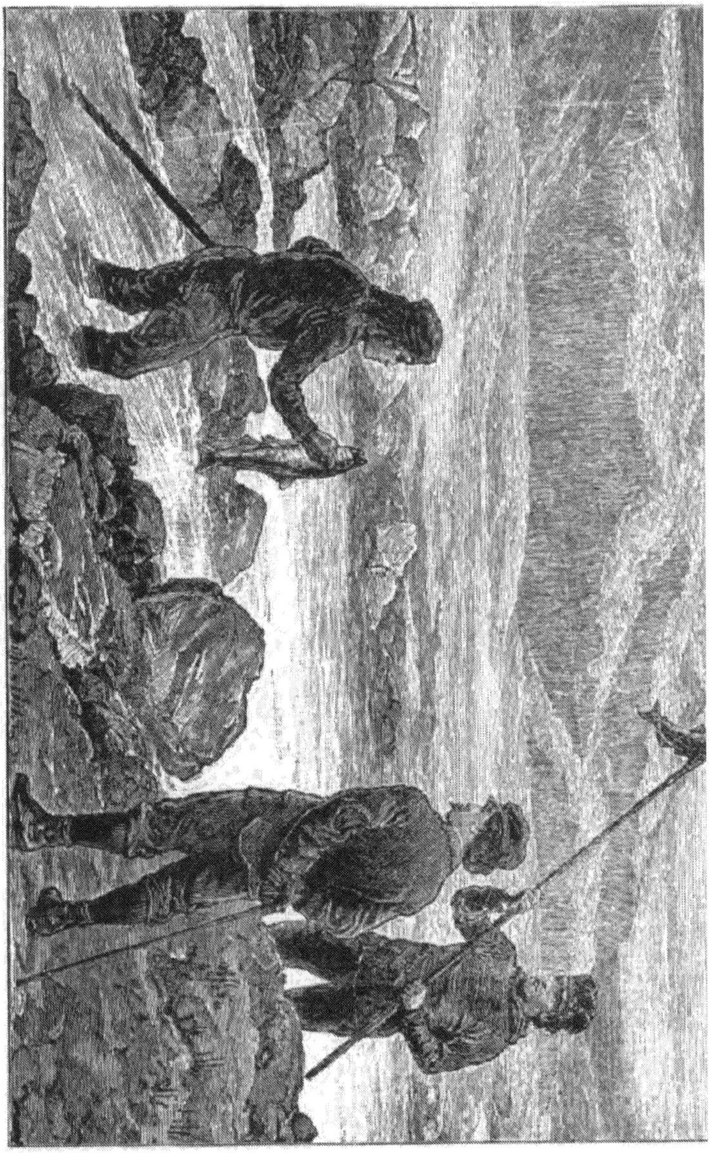

separately from the skin. The rear portion of the tent is made of the skins with the hairy side exposed, while the front is made of the transparent integument, or "mumme," which admits the light almost as freely as if made of ground glass. The skin portion is impervious to water, but the mumme admits the rain almost as readily as it does the light.

Seal-hunting is pursued after different methods, according to the time of the year and the nature of the ice, for upon or through the ice seals are nearly always killed. In the calm, genial days of spring they come up through their blow-holes, and enjoy a roll in the snow or a quiet nap in the sun. Their capture is then readily effected. The hunter steals as close as possible, say within four to one hundred yards, and cautiously lies down on a small bear-skin mat, which, as he moves, is dragged along, and kept under him as a protection against the cold and wet. He rests his weight chiefly upon his left hip, the knee bent, and the leg drawn up beneath him on the bear-skin mat. As long as the seal looks in his direction the hunter remains motionless, or raises his head and soon drops it upon his shoulder, uttering a noise like that of a seal blowing.

When, after a careful inspection, the seal is satisfied that no danger threatens, it drops its head upon the ice, and indulges in a few winks, but at the least noise or motion is again on the alert. The hunter profits by its nap to hitch himself along by means of his right foot and left hand, preserving all the while his recumbent position, and if detected by the seal, either stopping suddenly and blowing, or flopping around, like a seal enjoying a sun-bath, as he may consider advisable. Generally he contrives in this way to get near enough to bring down his victim with a rifle, or strike it with a seal-spear or " oo-nar." But sometimes, just as he is on the point of shooting or of spearing the seal, his hopes are frustrated, and the seal slips suddenly into the sea through its hole, on the very verge of which it rests, seldom straying beyond a foot or two from its secure asylum.

Mr. Gilder says that it is amusing to watch a seal's countenance, through a spy-glass, when a hunter is on the track. So intelligent and so human is the look that you can almost imagine the creature to be thinking. It will start up suddenly and gaze at the hunter, who, perhaps, is lying motionless, with an intense scrutiny that seems to say, "I am almost sure I saw *it* move that time, but I suppose I was mistaken!" Then, with a sleepy look, almost with a yawn, it lowers its head, and the hunter begins to hitch himself along again with slow and wary movement.

Suddenly up goes the seal's head, and so quickly that the hunter has no time to subside as before, but is forced to roll about, blowing off steam, and lifting his feet around just like a seal flapping its tail, so that at a little distance it is by no means easy to distinguish which is the seal and which the man. A smile then seems to overspread the creature's face, and you can fancy it saying to itself, " I caught him that time. What a fool I was to be frightened though! I thought it was a man, and it's only an ookjook."

At last the hunter gains the point whence he considers it safe to deliver his attack: you hear the report of his gun, and see him immediately spring to his feet and rush for his prey. The animal rarely escapes if the bullet strike its head or neck, though even then it sometimes slips out of reach, so close does it keep to its hole. But if hit anywhere else it generally eludes the hunter, though it may eventually perish of its wound. Often the hunter gains the hole in time to seize his prey by the hind flipper just as it is gliding down into the water. " I remember," says Gilder, " standing and gazing mournfully down into a hole one day, through which a seal that I had shot had just escaped, though his blood tinged the water and the edges of the ice, and while I was lamenting my ill-luck, I heard a splash behind me, and turned in time to see the seal come up through another hole. He looked awfully sick, and didn't see me until I had him by the flipper, sprawling on his back, at a safe distance from the hole. This was quite good luck for me, for such an opportunity rarely occurs. When struck with a spear," adds Gilder, " they seldom escape, for the line is fastened to the side of the spear-head, which detaches itself from the staff, and holds on to the flesh like a harpoon. Sometimes, however, the seal will slip away after the spear is thrown, and instead of sticking in him, it strikes the ice where he has been lying. This is very aggravating after the cold and tedious labour of working up to it has been accomplished; but the Eskimo bears his misfortune with equanimity. It is seldom that he says more than 'Ma-muk'-poo-now' (No good), or 'Mar-me-an'-nu' (which means 'angry,' or is an expression used when one is angry). He gathers up his weapons, sits down and lights his pipe, and, after a recuperative smoke, moves on in search of another opportunity to go through the same process."

The walrus, in the estimation of the Eskimo, ranks second only to the seal. Of the Innuits of North Hudson Bay and Melville Peninsula it is the staple food. It is in season nearly all the year—that is, all the time the natives are out hunting reindeer inland, in order to secure sufficient skins to make their winter clothing and sleeping blankets. The Kinnepatoos, who dwell in the neighbourhood of Chesterfield Inlet and its tributaries, appear to be the only, or almost the only tribe who live almost exclusively upon the reindeer; and these kill no more walrus and seal than are required to provide them with their summer attire of gloves and shoes. The Netchellik and Ookjoolik tribes live chiefly upon seals; and, as they are without firearms, they have scarcely any chance of killing reindeer when the thick frozen snow incrusts the ground. The Ooquusik-Sillik people, who dwell upon Back's Great Fish River and its tributary Hayes River, live almost wholly upon fish. The Iwilliks, who inhabit the coast of Hudson Bay from a point near the mouth of Chesterfield Inlet to Repulse Bay, the Igloolik, Amitigoke, Sekoselar, Akkolear, and, indeed, all the various tribes along the northern shore of Hudson Strait, Fox Channel, and Southampton Island, depend chiefly upon the walrus. It is one of the largest animals inhabiting the Arctic waters, and contains a large quantity of feeding material. A walrus of ordinary size weighs about ten or twelve hundred pounds; and as every particle of it is eaten, except the bones, it is necessarily regarded as a precious booty. The blood, blubber, intestines, even the hide, the undigested contents of the stomach, ay, and the softer bones, as well as the windpipe and œsophagus, are all eaten, either raw or cooked.

The walrus is usually met with near the edge of the ice-floe or shore-piece, unless in the vicinity there is a good deal of loose ice, and in that case it will generally be found on the larger cakes of loose ice. It is hunted in boats; or if the wind blows against the pack and keeps them on the floe, they can be successfully hunted afoot. The method pursued is exactly the same as in the case of the seal, except that the spear is preferred for the walrus and the rifle for the seal. Usually two hunters proceed to the attack together, one hiding behind the other, so as to appear but one. When the spear is thrown, both hold on to the line, which is coiled round their arms to cause the greatest possible amount of friction and exhaust the animal speedily. The head of the spear is made of walrus-tusk, and measures about three inches long and three inches thick. It has an iron barb, that is kept very sharp.

The line is attached to the middle of the spear-head, the near end being slanted, so that when the line is hauled tight it lies crosswise in the wound, like a harpoon, and cannot readily be extracted when it has once passed through the animal's tough hide. When the line is nearly run out, the end of the spear shaft is passed through a loop in the end of the line, and firmly secured by digging a little hole in the ice for the end of the spear to rest in, the foot resting upon the line, and against the shaft, to steady it. The hunter thus gains a great advantage over his powerful game; and when he is fortunate enough to get firm hold, the walrus has no chance of escape, unless the line should be cut against the edge of the sharp ice, or the thin ice break off, and hunter, line, and all be precipitated into the water. Sometimes, though much less frequently, the line gets entangled round the hunter's arm, so that he cannot cast it off; whereupon he is inevitably drawn into the sea, and, too often, drowned,—his knife being seldom at hand when wanted, and no amount of experience being sufficient to forewarn an Innuit against a possible danger.

The hunter is sometimes alone when he strikes a walrus, and in that case he need be dexterous to secure the spear-hold in the ice; or, if he fail to secure that advantage, he may sit down and brace his feet against a small hummock, and test his muscle against that of the walrus. In a contest of this kind, however, the walrus is generally victorious, though the Innuit always struggles on to the end, and is often dragged to the very brink of the ice before he can find a protuberance against which to steady his feet. Sometimes he is actually pulled down under the ice before he lets go. His tenacity is not so wonderful when we remember that if he loses the walrus he loses also his line and his harpoon.

Toogoolar, one of Lieutenant Schwatka's Eskimos, is described as a mighty walrus-hunter; but his success was partly due to his exceptional physical strength. When this Eskimo Samson is at one end of the line, with his feet steadied against a hummock, the walrus at the other has but little chance. Indeed, "the odds" are all the other way. Toogoolar appears to be popularly known as Oxeomadiddlee, just as Mr. Gladstone is popular amongst the British public as "the People's William," and Lord Beaconsfield was long known as "Dizzy." This singular name is an

Innuit expression of greeting, or rather an exclamation used when one arrives at any place, like the clown's "Here we are again!" How it originated is thus told :—

Several years ago he was hunting walrus on the pack-ice, when a sudden change of wind blew it out to sea; a contingency to which hunters are always exposed, and the greatest danger they incur in their adventurous calling. Many are thus carried away and are never again heard of; while others have been conveyed a long distance from their home before the drift again touched the shore-ice and allowed them to find their way back if possible. Sometimes they starve to death before the ice again lands, though, on the other hand, one hears of some marvellous escapes. As, for example, four Eskimos—namely, Equeesik, and his brother Owawork, Nanook, and Blucher—were carried off from Depot Island, with one of Lieutenant Schwatka's sledges, just before the departure of the expedition. They did not get back for four or five days, but experienced very little inconvenience. They built an igloo on the largest ice-cake they could reach, and as they had a dead walrus with them, had an ample supply of food. They made a lamp of walrus blubber, and burned the hide to warm their snow-hut. The ice-cake touched the shore below Chesterfield Inlet, when they jumped on the sledge and drove home.

When Toogoolar was borne off, he was absent so long a time that his tribe had abandoned all hope of seeing him again. However, one morning, during a severe snow-storm, he arrived in camp. No one had noticed his approach until, crawling through the doorway of an igloo, he stood among his friends, and exclaimed, "Ox'-e-o-ma-did'-dle-e" (Good morning. Here we are again!) From Repulse Bay he had been conveyed to the neighbourhood of Whale Point; but an easterly wind driving the pack on shore, he escaped, but had to make his way home on foot. He had his walrus line and spear with him, and had killed a walrus while on the pack; but the piece that held his food was broken off and floated away from him, so that for several days he had nothing to eat—an experience, however, of no novel character to an Innuit, who will fast for an exceptional period without injury.

When a walrus is killed, some time is consumed in cutting it up and preparing it for removal to camp. Generally there are several helpers in attendance on any hunter who carries a line and spear.

And some will walk along the edge of the pack until they meet with a countryman working up to a walrus, or a party engaged in dividing their booty.

It is the custom among the Innuits that all who are present when a walrus is cut up shall have a share of it; a custom which generally insures a numerous attendance. The hunter, however, takes his share first, and this is usually one of the hind quarters, or both hind flippers, and the head always. The head is the *bonne bouche;* and Mr. Gilder declares there is nothing more palatable during the Arctic winter and spring than raw frozen walrus head and tongue. Though not attractive in appearance, it is, he says, most enjoyable. The meat is hard, but not particularly tough (for walrus), and consists of alternate layers of lean and fat. It is eaten with an accompaniment of seal blubber, and is generally the occasion of a common feast for all the men in the camp. The women are made welcome to whatever is left, but are never allowed to eat with the men; and if the banquet takes place in a small igloo, even the females who belong to it are expelled until their lords and masters have satisfied their appetites.

The arrival of a sledge-load of walrus meat in an Eskimo camp, or among a party of Arctic explorers, is the most cheerful sight which a traveller can behold; nor is his admiration of it diminished by the fact that his own is one of the hungry stomachs to be benefited by the welcome booty. The women catch sight of the coming sledge in the distance, and immediately light their big stone lamps and put on their kettles, and make everything ready to cook the meat as soon as it arrives. Not a second is wasted. The cooking is seldom done in each igloo separately; but the Innuit with the largest kettle, or the biggest heart, stands at the door of his hut as soon as the viand is ready, and cries aloud, "O-yook, o-yook!" or "Warm food;" and lo! all the men and boys hurry to the spot, each armed with a knife, and fall-to eagerly, without further preface. The Innuit, however, eats most of his food raw; and *o-yooks* are really festival occasions, though they often occur several times in the same day, and may take place at any time of the day or the night, when the natives are assembled in their villages, and have in hand a good supply of food. It is in such happy seasons of abundance that they compensate themselves for by-gone times of severe privation.

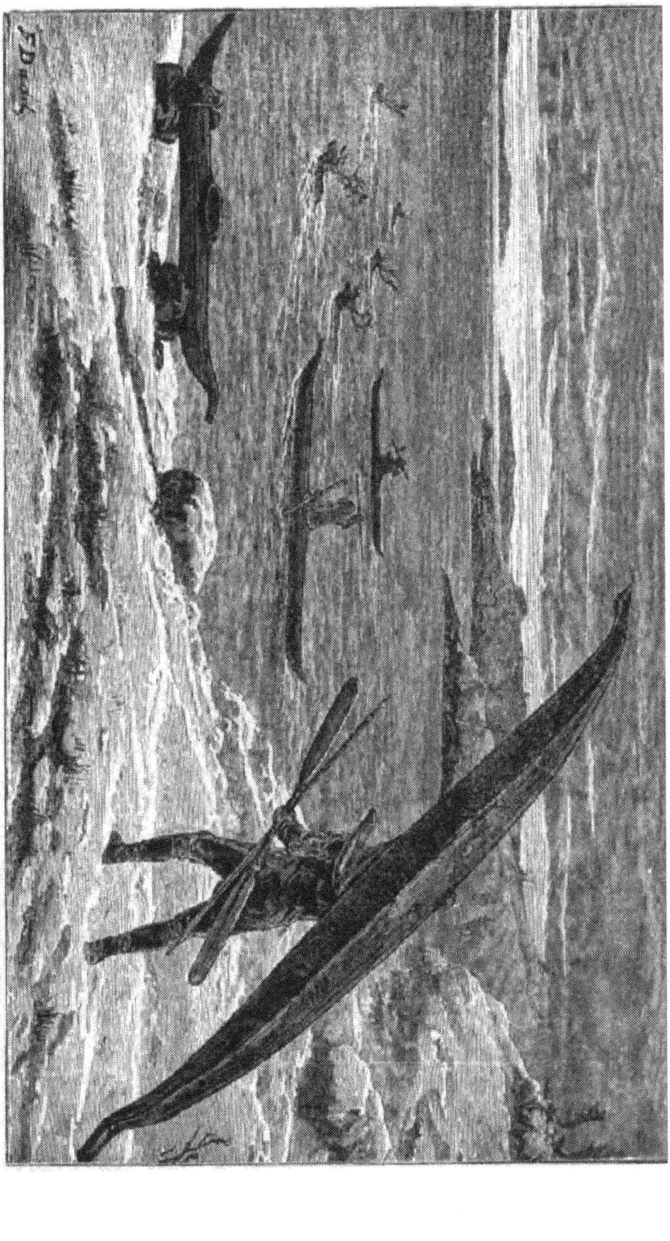

Reindeer hunting is also much practised among the Innuits. Driving the animals into the sea, they pursue them in their light kayaks; and when they are exhausted with swimming, readily make booty of them.

CHAPTER V

SAFE HOME.

AT length the time came for the homeward voyage of Lieutenant Schwatka and his gallant companions. On the 7th of August 1880, the whaling-ship *George and Mary* set sail from Marble Island, and made toward Whale Point, so as to hail any other vessels that had come into Hudson Bay, and ascertain what news they brought. They found large quantities of ice in Daly Bay and the entrance to Rorer's Welcome, a bridge or causeway of solid ice still stretching from near Whale Point to Southampton Island.

On Sunday, the 8th, while slowly pushing through the ice-pack off Cape Fullerton, they saw a she-bear and cub asleep on a large cake of ice about a quarter of a mile from the ship, and lowered one of the boats to give chase. The bears seemed at once to scent danger, and took to the water, the old one in the depth of her maternal affection for her cub carrying it on her back. When they found the boat gaining upon them, and close at hand, they abandoned the water and stood at bay on a cake of ice. Lieutenant Schwatka fired; his bullet struck the she-bear's back-bone, and down she dropped. Mr. Williams put an end to her misery by shooting her through the head. The cub they were anxious to take alive; but the poor little creature clung to its mother's bleeding body with painful fidelity. It was quite pathetic to see its efforts to cover her with its own little form,—to see it lick her face and wounds,—occasionally rising on its hind legs and growling a fierce defiance of its enemies. At this juncture Lieutenant Schwatka sprang upon the ice, and after several ineffectual attempts at last succeeded in throwing a rope over the head of the cub, which was towed alongside the ship and hoisted on deck, together with its mother's carcass.

The remainder of their voyage home was unmarked by any interesting incident. On Tuesday, August 20th, "Land ho!" was shouted from the mast-head, and soon to those on board the *George and Mary* became plainly visible the low white shores of the island of Nantucket. Before Wednesday night they had landed in New Bedford, "safe and sound," after all their adventurous and perilous experiences.

CHAPTER VI.

LIEUTENANT SCHWATKA'S PERSONAL NARRATIVE.

THE foregoing relation has been condensed from an exhaustive statement by Colonel Gilder which appeared during the months of September and October 1880 in the *New York Herald*. The reader, however, may be glad to hear what was said by Lieutenant Schwatka, the commander of the expedition, to whose prudence and resolution its success was mainly due. On the 28th of October he was publicly received and congratulated by the American Geographical Society, and, in reply to their vote of thanks, he delivered an address, of which the following is a summary:—

"On the morning of April 1, 1879," he said, "we dragged our sledges on the salt-water ice near Camp Daly, and, shaking hands, bade our trusty Innuit friends good-bye, and stopped a moment to take a last look at the dreary, cheerless mass of snow domes that had been our home for eight long months. There is something peculiarly depressing in starting upon a long, unknown venture, especially if a person has upon his mind all the cares and duties of a commander, to warn him that in case of misfortune (which he must avert) he alone does not suffer. And this was an expedition wherein misfortune might easily befall us. With less than one month's provisions we were separating ourselves by an icy desert of eight hundred or nine hundred miles from all chances of rescue, with seventeen human and forty-two brute mouths to be fed, in a country reported destitute of game." After describing the component members of his party, and adding that they carried ten American breech-loaders of different patterns, and over ten thousand rounds of ammunition, he continued:—The route was to be directly across land, in a north-west direction, to the nearest available point on Back River; thence to King William Land. Crossing the course of the Wager River, which, though marked on the charts, appeared to be non-existent, they travelled over a very hilly and even mountainous country at the rate of ten to fifteen miles a day. "Our greatest obstacle was the well-known tempestuous weather of the Arctic regions. We had an almost uninterrupted storm from the 20th of April to the 1st of June—forty-three days." Following up a tributary of Back River, which he named Hayes River, they came, at about forty miles from its mouth, on a small Eskimo village of about thirty souls, only two of whom had ever before seen a white man. The elder of these gave much interesting information of a lost *kodloonah*, or white man's ship, which he had personally visited some thirty years before, eight miles due west of Grant Point. This, of course, was one of Sir John Franklin's ships, which had floated down Victoria Channel, after its abandonment off Victory Point, King William Land. The story told by the old Eskimo ran as follows :—

He remembered Lieutenant Back, who explored the Great Fish River in 1834, and minutely described his meeting with him at the Dangerous Rapids. The next white man he saw was a dead one, in a large ship eight miles off Grant Point. The body was in a bunk in the after-part of the vessel, which had "four big sticks," one pointing out, and the others standing up. A small boat hung from the davits; this they cut down. Some three or four of the ship's sails were set. Many empty casks were found on board. A large pile of dirt on one side of the cabin door on the snow showed that the cabin had been recently swept out. On the mainland were tracks of white men who had probably been hunting for deer. He saw the ship in the spring, before the spring snows fell, and the tracks in the fresh spring snows of the same year, about the time the young reindeer come (June). The white men he never saw, but thought they lived in the ship until the autumn, and then removed to the mainland. The natives did not understand how to enter the vessel, so they cut an entrance through one side; and when the ice melted in the summer, in poured the water, and the ship sank, only her masts remaining above the surface. Shortly after this event, they found a small boat in Wilmot Bay; but they never met with any cairns or monuments erected by the white men. Among the relics of Sir John Franklin's expedition collected by Lieutenant Schwatka was a small board, apparently a bunk board, which once formed a permanent part of the wrecked vessel, and was stripped from it by the Eskimos. On one side were the initials "L. F.," designed by the heads of copper tacks of the old style.

Lieutenant Schwatka, continuing his personal recital, said that on the 31st of May he encountered a large village of Netchellik Eskimos in the bay to the west of Richardson Point, containing about one hundred men, women, and children. The information they gave proved beyond doubt the complete destruction of the more important records of Sir John Franklin's expedition, at a point three miles to the northwest, which Lieutenant Schwatka named Starvation Cove. There, too, the Netchelliks discovered a small boat on its keel, with skeletons in and around it; probably the small boat spoken of by Dr. Rae, Sir Leopold M'Clintock, and Captain Hall, all of whom estimated the number of the dead at from forty to fifty. The Eskimos, however, who had been eye-witnesses of the sad scene, reduced it to from six to ten.

The following passage must be taken for what it is worth, according to the reader's own judgment:—

"The most important information connected with this boat place, which is evidently the farthest reached by any body of Franklin's men in 1848, is that concerning a sealed tin box, about two feet long, and about one foot square at the ends, which was broken open by the natives and found to contain books, and a small piece of iron to which all pieces of the same material would adhere when brought in contact.* This tin box was retained by the Netchelliks, and its contents emptied on the ground, where they slowly perished. Some few of them were given to their children for playthings. In this box was also a small box containing human bones that had been sawn in two in order to extract the marrow, thus showing that they had been reduced to the most distressing and terrible condition in order to prolong life.† That men thus placed should have burdened themselves with such a quantity of books, and the careful manner of their preservation, shows an importance which can only be attributed to the records of the expedition. I think it not improbable that the magnetized iron spoken of by these people, from its description, was the dip-needle with which the north magnetic pole had been re-determined, their beset condition in its vicinity giving them unusual opportunities to narrow this interesting problem within closer limits than could have been done by Ross, its discoverer, in his hasty sledge-journey in 1831. This instrument would be a valuable historical relic."

During the summer months, the party, as we have

* See *ante*, p. 42.
† This seems most improbable. Why should the bones have been preserved in a tin box?

CROSSING SIMPSON STRAIT IN KAYAKS.
Page 105

already seen, were engaged in a thorough search of King William Land and the adjacent mainland, pushing forward from Camp Daly to the shores of Simpson Strait,—an inlet which they crossed in the Eskimo kayaks on the 17th of September. Their store of "civilized food" was exhausted by June 24th, and thenceforward, until March 20, 1880, the white men lived in the same manner as their native allies, principally on the flesh of the reindeer, five hundred and eleven of which were killed by the explorers and their auxiliaries. The search began on the fourth day of July, when the snow had sufficiently disappeared; at which date they were at Cape Felix, King William Land, near which point the *Erebus* and *Terror* had been ice-bound in September 1846. From Cape Felix to Collinson Inlet, that is, over fifteen to twenty-five miles of coast-line, they carried on their search from June 27th to July 24th, traversing not fewer than two hundred and seventy-eight miles,—the work being done most carefully and exhaustively, and carried to a considerable distance inland. This littoral strip was of high importance, because it was the land nearest to the two imprisoned vessels during their prolonged captivity. But though two cairns were found, they revealed no secrets. Under the base stones of one lay hidden a sheet of letter paper, inscribed with the drawing of a hand, the index finger of which apparently pointed southward. It was in too decayed a state for the writing to be deciphered. A large number of interesting relics was found here (of which we have already given a sufficient description). In the indentation of the coast which Lieutenant Schwatka, in allusion to Lieutenant Irving's grave, called Irving Bay, the record left by Captain M'Clintock was met with. Some stockings were also found, roughly made out of blankets, pointing to a want of necessary clothing. Returning southward, the explorers discovered and interred a partial skeleton near Franklin Point; and another, which from the fine quality of the clothing and linen, the buttons, and other signs, they took to be that of an officer, was re-buried in a desecrated grave on Point-le-Vesconte. Near a despoiled grave on Payer Point was found a skull, with a belt-buckle and a musket cap. Some four or more skeletons at the boat place in South Erebus Bay received decent interment. The general drift of all this evidence goes to prove that the boat and the sledge on which it rested had floated to this point from the sea: hence it must have been abandoned on the ice, probably when the ice broke up in Victoria Channel in the summer of 1848. When

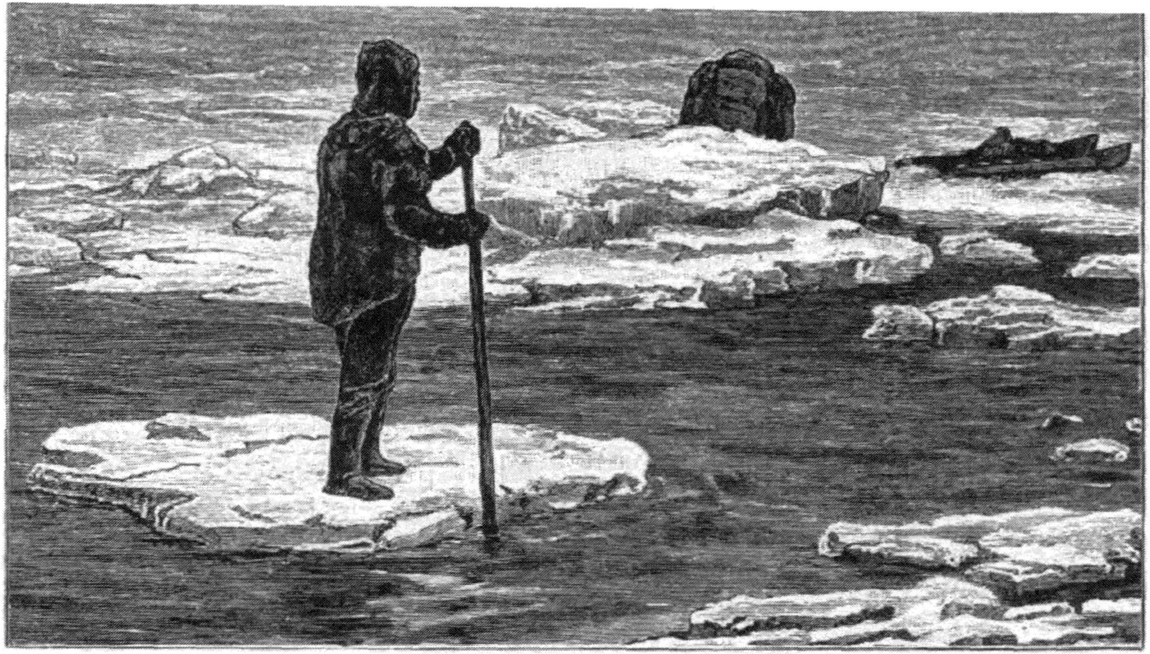

BREAKING UP OF THE ICE.

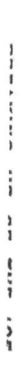

the Schwatka expedition was in this vicinity the disruption of the great frozen fields did not take place until July the 24th. After that, sledging had to be given up, and consequently the party were laboriously occupied until August 1st in conveying their *impedimenta* from Erebus to Terror Bay.

Little of interest was met with until they reached Tulloch Point, where the natives pointed out the remains of a solitary skeleton. "After re-burial, as had been done at all such places, a rock monument was erected to designate the spot. A painfully interesting circumstance is shown in the rough construction of this grave from small stones, although larger and better adapted ones were in the immediate vicinity, differing in a marked degree from all previous graves encountered, thus showing the rapidly waning strength of the few survivors."

Lieutenant Schwatka proceeded to state that he had hoped the return winter journey would have occupied little more than a month; but a combination of adverse circumstances prevented him from reaching Camp Daly until the 4th of March 1880. This return journey we have already described. (See p. 66.) The coldest weather encountered by the expedition was 71° F., on the 3rd of January; the average for that month, which was the coldest, being 53° 2' F. "I was pleased," says the lieutenant, "to note the perfect acclimatization of the white men of the party, who suffered no more than the Eskimos under similar circumstances. Reaching Camp Daly, I was confronted with the unexpected fact that Captain Thomas F. Barry, master of the *Eothen*, who had been intrusted with all of our remaining provisions and a large quantity of other material, had stolen them in his departure from Hudson Bay." It is scarcely needful to add that Captain Barry has put forward a very different statement. There can be no doubt, however, that his negligence or greed, whichever it was, placed the courageous adventurers in a very difficult position, and that their sufferings must have been extreme had they not been generously received and relieved by Captain M. A. Baker, of the whaling-ship *George and Mary* of New Bedford.

This expedition is memorable for having achieved the longest sledge journey ever made, both as regards *time* and *distance*. It was absent from its base of operations eleven months and twenty days, and traversed 2819 geographical, or 3251 statute miles. It was the first expedition which deliberately and systematically placed its reliance, for the support of its human members and its draught animals, on the game of the country, and spread its experience in this respect continuously over every month of the year. It was the first, moreover, in which the white men lived wholly, and of their own free will, on the same food as their Eskimo allies. So well and so thoroughly did it do its work, that, probably, we may venture the assertion that not a single member of Franklin's expedition now lies with bleached bones on the inhospitable snow; for each a decent grave has been dug. Where nature had not anticipated their efforts, or Franklin's retreating crews had not themselves performed the last sad office, and paid the last sad tribute of respect to their comrades, it was discharged by Lieutenant Schwatka and his followers. From the incomplete condition of the skeletons, their inextricable confusion, and the wide area over which they were scattered, it was difficult to compute with any certainty the number interred, and while some estimated it as high as forty, others placed it as low as seventeen.

As Dr. Hayes, himself distinguished in the annals of Arctic exploration, remarked, on the occasion of Lieutenant Schwatka's reception, we now know all that we shall ever know of the fate of the one hundred and twenty-nine men who went forth, buoyant and strong, to play their heroic part in that great drama of Polar exploration which had long been their country's pride. The problem which engaged the loving perseverance of Lady Franklin, and the energy and effort of so many gallant and generous spirits, has been solved. We know *how* the explorers perished, and *where*, and, with some reasonable degree of certainty, *when*. All honour to their memories! They and their brave leaders deserved well of the commonwealth. It is the legacy of example and inspiration which such men bequeath that makes a nation rich.

CHAPTER VII.

THE VOYAGE OF THE "JEANNETTE."

DR. HAYES, we may add, alluded to the voyage of the *Jeannette*, of which we shall now offer a very brief account, dismissing Lieutenant Schwatka to take his place high among the men who have battled with perils of the Polar wastes.

The *Jeannette* was fitted out by an American citizen, who had kept his eye steadily fixed upon the North Pole, as a goal to which human effort might even yet attain, and with a liberality and enthusiasm scarcely matched even in the annals of Polar enterprise, he equipped this vessel for the purpose of discovery. She had been built specially for Arctic cruising, for contending with the "floes" and "fields," and had proved her strength and fitness in three voyages. But her new owner caused her to be materially strengthened and entirely repaired; and when she left San Francisco in July 1879, she had on board every convenience for health and comfort that experience and scientific skill could suggest. She carried an ample supply of provisions for three years. Her immediate destination was Wrangell Land. This shore, named after the Russian explorer, Admiral Wrangell, was never actually seen by him during the four monotonous years he spent on the Siberian coast of Asia, near the mouth of the Kolyma river; but the natives apprised him that they had often seen and even visited it. Wrangell's attempts to push his researches in that direction were always baffled, even in February, by open water, the Polynia of the Russians, which was found to extend north and west to the New Siberian Islands, for there it was discovered by Wrangell's co-explorer, Lieutenant Anjou Urangello. This far northern shore, hidden away in the cold gray Arctic atmosphere, has, however, been frequently sighted by adventurous whalers in propitious open seasons, and traced to a considerable distance in a north-easterly direction. Whalers, the reader may be told, never intentionally enter the ice; they skirt its margin, where the whales abound, and catch glimpses of the land only by accident and on rare occasions. The *Jeannette*, on the other hand, was despatched to push its way *into* the ice—should such exist—at the most open point, and to fight and wrestle until it reached Wrangell Land.

She sailed, as we have said, in July 1879, under the command of Captain de Long, and very soon after her departure passed into a mystery almost as complete as that which once surrounded the Franklin expedition. When the summer of 1880 came, and no news of her whereabouts could anywhere be learned, considerable anxiety was necessarily excited, and the less sanguine or less well-informed spirits began to apprehend that, like so many of her predecessors, she had perished — that one more pitiful holocaust had been offered up to the potent "demon of the North."

In the summer of 1880 the *Corwin* went in search of the missing vessel. She brought back no information of her whereabouts, but some interesting particulars of that Arctic life with which we are now growing so familiar.

In the early part of the month of August the *Corwin* cruised in the vicinity of Cape Saline and Herald Island, pushing her way through a labyrinth of ice-floes. There is something singularly blank and cheerless in the aspect of these shores—a dense mist generally rests upon the heights, and the cliffs frown like a rampart of iron on the approaching vessel. All around, the sea is heavy with thick packs of ice, which frequently hurtle against each other with a resounding crash; and the monotony of the scene is relieved only by the appearance of troops of wild geese winnowing the air with rapid wings, or of shoals of whales rising to the surface with a sudden commotion.

Forty miles to the south of Behring Strait lies a mass of rock, discovered by Captain Cook, and named by him, with superfluous loyalty, King Island. Its cliffs are almost perpendicular on every side, and rise to an elevation of seven hundred and fifty feet. The water is of depth sufficient to allow a big ship to approach them very closely. This lonely Arctic stronghold of the deep has a bold, rude outline; and its surface consists principally of rock, scantily clothed with mosses and lichens. Grass there is not, nor shrub, nor tree. A curious feature is presented by the occurrence, on the most elevated points, of some rude stone pillars, which the voyagers of the *Corwin* compare to the remains of a Druidical temple, like Stonehenge, or the ruins of some ancient feudal stronghold. But the visitor's attention is principally attracted by an Eskimo village, composed chiefly of "houses excavated in the rocks, on a slope of somewhat less than 45°, and from one to two hundred feet above the sea." In the distance it might be taken for a colony of sea-fowl, of some of those species which choose for their breeding-places the lonely islands of the North. That human beings should locate themselves in such a dreary spot may seem wonderful. The explanation is to be found in the one word—*walrus*. These animals abound in the surrounding seas, and in large numbers make their appearance on the ice-packs and the island rocks. As the voyagers clambered up the rocky ascent to the Eskimo settlement, they saw one or more walrus-skins and portions of the entrails stretched to dry in front of nearly every house. Men were busily engaged in cleaning the white ivory tusks, women in splitting the fresh skin, unconscious of, or undisturbed by, the greasy stench that polluted the air.

The interior of the houses, or caves, is spoken of as being "rank, greasy, and stuffy beyond description;" as something which to the perceptions of our fashionable *æsthetes* would be terribly repulsive. The furniture consists of furs, skins, fishing and hunting tackle, and walrus meat. The decoration is reduced to the simplicity of "unpleasant odours;" or, to put it more briefly and plainly, the essentials consist of walrus and the accessories of bad smells. Coleridge affirmed that Cologne boasted of two-and-seventy separate stenches; King's Island has the advantage over Cologne in possessing only one stench, the all-pervading scent of walrus. To the simple occupant we may opine that a King's Island house is a proper Elysium; but to one whose ideas have been inspired by "Art at Home" professors, it would appear, we fancy, a miserable and squalid den. Says the *Corwin's* chronicler:—"At one house we visited, on invitation of the owner, he, in order to be hospitable, had set out a great delicacy—a wooden tray full of walrus heart. I am generally not very backward in eating what is set before me, but on this occasion the melancholy consciousness of a stomach obliged me to decline the proffered hospitality. Not so backward, however, was our Eskimo interpreter, who for some weeks had been living on the Government ration of 'salt horse' and hard tack. It would have done your heart good to see how he reverted to first principles. Near the village is a cave, used by the natives as a storehouse or crypt for food, the entrance to which is not unlike an immense gable window."

The *Corwin*, in the course of her voyage, touched

at many of the places visited and named by our countrymen during the various expeditions sent out in search of Sir John Franklin. Among those may be mentioned Emma Harbour, on the Siberian coast, where Captain Moore wintered in the *Plover* in 1848-49. It is enclosed by lofty, barren mountains, which lift their desolate summits on high among the clouds, and seem to be built up of broken boulders and fragments of rock. On the American coast, the western extremity of the New World, the farthest point of the great continent, Cape Prince of Wales terminates in a bold, rugged promontory, the famous peak of which, being connected with the mainland by a low range of hills, seems at a distance to stand isolated amid the wild ocean-waters. Near the head of Kotzebue Sound, and almost directly under the Arctic Circle, the *Corwin's* voyagers found, on Chamisso Island, about two hundred feet above the sea-level, an astronomical station, composed of a mound of earth and a pile of stones, on the top of which rose a wooden shaft, about twelve feet high, bearing carved inscriptions of several English vessels—the *Blossom*, the *Herald*, the *Plover*. To these was promptly added the name of " the *Corwin*, 1880." The voyagers fell in with an almost intelligible record, referring to a bottle buried twenty feet to the magnetic north, but were compelled to abandon their search by the attacks of swarms of mosquitoes. Captain Kellett's party, of H.M.S. *Plover*, report having found here, in July 1849, the cask of flour left by Beechy twenty-three years before, and that it was quite perfect. The sand around it was frozen so hard that the cask was not extracted without much difficulty.

Detached from Chamisso is a steep, broken rock, incessantly echoing with the clang of tumultuous waves, known as Puffin Island, from the myriads of ocean-birds which find a shelter there during their period of incubation.

While lying at anchor off Chamisso, some of the voyagers made an excursion to a spot of considerable zoological interest, Elephant Point, the origin and formation of which have been the subject of conflicting statements. According to Kotzebue, it is a mass of ice covered with soil a foot thick, and containing an abundance of mammoth bones.* But Captain Beechy thinks that the appearance which induced Kotzebue to characterize it as an iceberg was produced either by the water of the thawing ice or snow

---

* The mammoth (*Elephas primogenius*) is now extinct, but formerly abounded in Northern Asia, and over the whole of Europe.

trickling down the earthy surface from above, or by the snow being accumulated against the cliff or collected in hollows during the winter, and afterwards converted into ice by a process of partial thaw and regelation. The upper soil, gradually loosened by the thaw, thus came, in course of time, to project itself over the cliff. Captain Hooper of the *Corwin* explored the place very thoroughly, and was rewarded by the discovery of almost the entire skeleton of a mammoth, the remains of an aurochs, a musk-ox, and the skull of an animal which he could not identify.

On the 25th of August the voyagers visited Point Barrow, in lat. 71° 23′ 31″ N., and long. 156° 21′ 30″ W.; a remote spot, seldom touched at by any navigator, and never before visited by a United States vessel. This, the western terminus of the American coast, as well as the north-westmost extreme of the American continent, is seldom accessible by boats even in the open season, on account of the ice which the strong northerly current here packs up to an immense height, fortifying the cape in such a manner that any advance towards it is attended by no little peril. "Figure to yourself a spit of coarse, dark brown sand and gravel, extending some six or eight miles from the regular coast-line, and having near its extremity, which is broader than any other part, several small lakes, generally frozen over by the end of August, and on the eastern side of this peninsula a large Eskimo village:......then may you form an incomplete notion of the topography of Point Barrow." Of the village and its inhabitants little need be said. They are Eskimos, and what more can be stated? Except, indeed, that they seem to approach nearer than any of their congeners to the supposed primitive man and old original cave-dweller in the construction of their houses, and are, if possible, more miserable and dirty. In their architectural work the whale's bones play an important part. Its lower jaw-bone and ribs form a support and framework for the covering of sod. One of the huts was composed of whale-skulls, with a roof of turf.

"In taking a stroll through the village," says our informant, "for the purpose of sight-seeing, we were asked not to go further in a certain direction, for fear of disturbing a sick man, who was at that moment being subjected to the magic spells and rites of the 'shaman' for the purpose of averting the malign influence of the Evil Spirit. On being told that one of our party was a medical man and a real 'shaman,' a native led the way to the sick man's igloo, and, requesting us to stop a short distance off, went to the house and interrupted the heathen exorcisms, which could now be distinctly heard as the convulsive utterances of a superstitious and ignorant savage in a condition of forced epilepsy. Permission to see the patient being soon given, an examination showed him to be suffering from hemiplegia and a skin disease known as rupia. After rendering the little medical assistance that lay in our power, we left him to the tender mercies of the 'shaman,' not, however, without a regret at being unable to see the operations and ceremonies of this individual, who may be regarded not so much as a cheat as a psychological phenomenon. Notwithstanding much that is wretched and forbidding among these people, they seem to have their share of domestic tranquillity, and one sees in them much to admire."

The Eskimos, as we know, are wofully deficient in almost everything that civilization has taught us to value and appreciate; but the deficiency has not affected their cheerful and genial disposition. Ignorance, with them, is bliss. Some observers find in them a strong likeness to the Australian aborigines. They are constantly gay and light of heart, full of smiles, and prompt of laughter, without gloom or moroseness. It is true, however, that they are excessively selfish, as most savage races are, the struggle for life apparently developing in them a strong feeling of self-love. Like the French, they are peculiarly sensitive to ridicule.

The appearance of white men anywhere in the neighbourhood of an Eskimo settlement is the general signal for the skin canoes to swarm off towards them with the entire family—*mit kind und regel*—and frequently with the dogs and even the household effects. It is the habit of the men to wear a tabret in the under lip, which is pierced for the purpose. "It looks so heathenish to see what would otherwise be good-looking features distorted by the contents of a stone quarry, which have been shaped into the form of an immense sleeve-button." The women are liberally tattooed; one who went on board the *Corwin* wore a bunch of coloured beads suspended from her nose. As for their babies, they are carried on the mother's back, and under her clothes, which form a kind of pouch, and from this heap a tiny head is generally protruding over one or the other shoulder. If a stranger come in sight, however, it retires, like a snail or a marsupial, into its cozy shelter. When the mother wishes to remove it, she bends forward, simultaneously passing her left hand up the back under her garments, and, catching hold of the child's feet, she pulls it downward to the left; next, sliding her right hand under the front part of her dress, she again seizes the feet, and in this fashion extracts her living burden.

The Eskimo, like most, if not all, savages, is very partial to dancing. One day, when the *Corwin* was in the vicinity of the place known among whalemen as "the Graveyard,"* because a fleet of whaling-vessels was abandoned there in 1871, some natives visited her, and, after a kindly reception, amused themselves with songs and dances. One of the songs resembled a monotonous chant, another had in it something of a waltz tune.

Our authority does not speak very favourably of their hospitality. According to Captain Beechy, he was offered at Cape Thompson the entrails of a fine seal and a bowl of coagulated blood, and when these failed to tempt his appetite, some narwhal cut into small bits was placed before him. At Point Hope the voyager we are quoting was offered by an Eskimo a portion of the meat he was eagerly devouring— some whale-meat that was very "high," and probably

* Near Point Belcher.

in flavour was as rank as in smell it was offensive. Whale, however, when fresh is, as the Scotchman said of Mrs. Siddons's acting, "nae so bad;" and there are whaler captains who eat it every morning for breakfast, prepared like codfish balls. The Eskimo apparently thrives on the flesh of whale and seal and walrus, eating it without salt; at times the supply is deficient, and then he is exposed to the most deplorable privation. Our authority learned from the Tschutschi at Plover Bay, on the Siberian coast, that many of their people had starved to death during the two previous winters. One of them, when asked why he did not go to kill walrus, which seemed very plentiful, replied curtly, but significantly, "Ah, big water, little canoe!"

So mild and inoffensive are the Eskimos that they rarely indulge in quarrelling, and their language, it is said, contains no words capable of giving expression to the stronger passions. They are reputed to be generally honest and truthful, though one of their number, who boarded the *Corwin* at the Diomede Islands, had an unfavourable opinion of the veracity of some of his countrymen. An individual of effusive disposition, he stepped up to the captain jauntily, and said, "My name's Dick; what's yours?" He went on to say that the people of East Cape, on the Siberian side, had informed him of the recent passage of a Russian man-of-war; but added, epigrammatically, "I believe he lie—East Cape." A bag of ship's bread was given to Dick, who soon exhausted his limited stock of whaleman's English, and some tobacco being exchanged for a few articles of native workmanship, he was dismissed. His pithy verdict on the East Capers became a household word among the *Corwin's* crew, so that, when allusion was made to any person's facility of invention or power of exaggeration, it was customary to say, "Oh, he's from East Cape."

The *Corwin* pursued her voyage in the direction of Wrangell Land and Herald Island, but without making any important contribution to our stock of geographical knowledge.

THE END.

Lightning Source UK Ltd.
Milton Keynes UK
UKHW020615071119
353079UK00005B/445/P